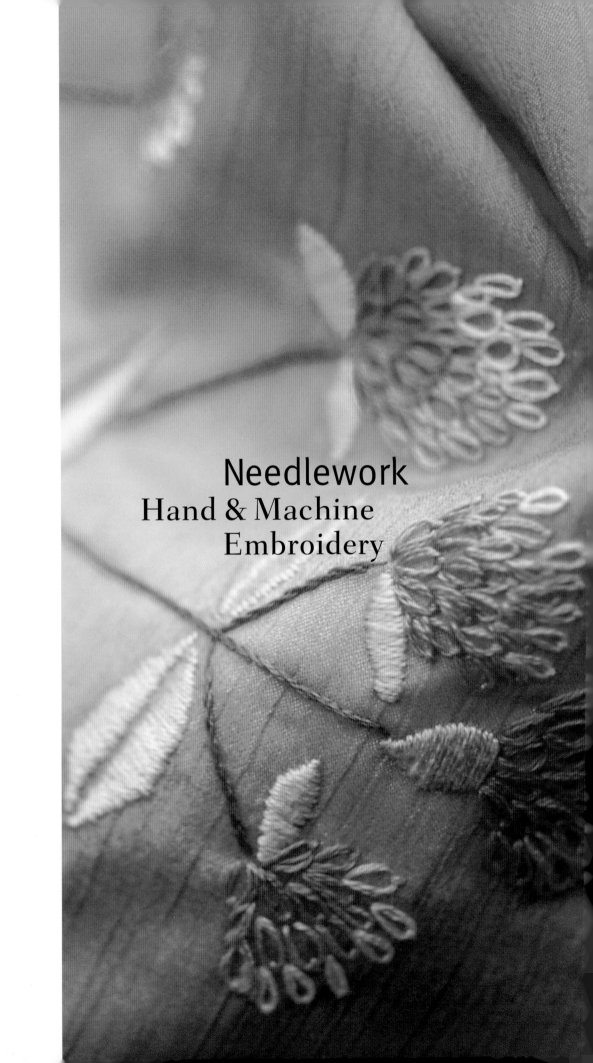

Needlework
Hand & Machine
Embroidery

Jacqueline Farrell

Needlework
Hand & Machine
Embroidery

HAMLYN

NEEDLE WORK
HAND & MACHINE EMBROIDERY

First published in 1998 by Hamlyn
an imprint of Reed Consumer Books Limited
Michelin House, 81 Fulham Road
London, SW3 6RB
and Auckland and Melbourne

Publishing Director LAURA BAMFORD

Executive Editor MIKE EVANS
Senior Editor NINA SHARMAN
Managing Editor CAROLINE BINGHAM

Art Director KEITH MARTIN
Executive Art Editor MARK WINWOOD
Designer LISA TAI
Production BONNIE ASHBY

Photography DAVID LOFTUS
Illustrations KATE SIMUNEK

The publishers have made every effort to
ensure that all instructions given in this book
are accurate and safe, but they cannot accept
liability for any resulting injury, damage or loss
to either person or property whether direct or
consequential and howsoever arising. The
author and publishers will be grateful for any
information which will assist them in keeping
future editions up-to-date.

A CIP record for this book is available from
the British Library.

ISBN 0 600 59510 2

Produced by Toppan Printing Co Ltd
Printed and bound in China

Contents

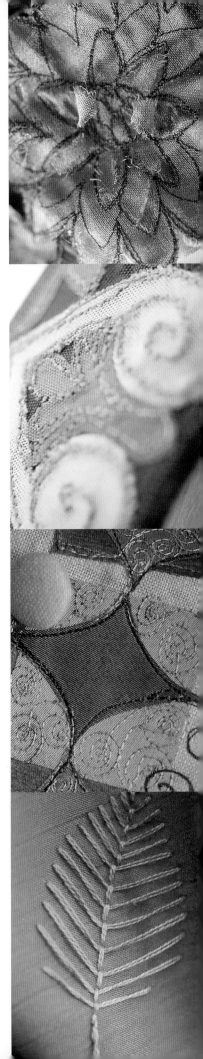

This book is designed to appeal to novice and experienced embroiderers alike. The design themes – Flowers and Gardens, City and Architecture, Sea and Sky, Global and Ethnic, and Food – were chosen because of the broad appeal and the richness and availability of each subject. It is important to find inspiration from a variety of sources as it makes an embroidered project more interesting and stretches and challenges your skills.

Some images and themes are easier to design from than others and I personally enjoy using natural forms and architecture as my starting point, but it is always exciting to see how other designers are inspired.

introduction

Above: *Bouquet brooches, page 26.*
Opposite page: above left –
Naive heart cushion, page 92;
above right – *Nautical tablecloth, page 56;*
below left – *Fruit motif shelf edging, page 106;*
below right – *Indian evening bag, page 78.*

I have chosen specific techniques for each project because every type of embroidery lends itself to a different look and timescale.

The more traditional hand embroidery stitches can be a little time-consuming but the finished effect has surface texture and colour combined, as well as adding an heirloom quality to the final piece.

Machine embroidery has developed in the last 15 years as domestic machines have become more sophisticated yet easier to operate. Ideas can be realized quickly and either solid colours or fine detail can be stitched. Fabric manipulation techniques such as fraying and pintucking add an extra dimension to the piece.

I hope that you find the projects in the book fresh and inspirational and that they will give you the confidence to take your own ideas further.

flowers and gardens

A natural palette of the organic tones and textures of flowers offers a fascinating and infinite source of design ideas that is perfect for translation into embroidery.

Above: *Seed pods are alive with a multitude of exciting design possibilities – look at this poppy's 10-point star.*
Opposite page: top left *– The softly focused outlines of this striking yellow flower already look as though they have been trapped between layers of chiffon;*
top right *– Strong veining on these flower heads adds a definition and shape ideal for a structured appliqué on crisp linen;*
below left *– The sugary pastels of the sweet pea are ideal for development into cross stitch motifs;*
below right *– The more abstract an image the more free the interpretation can be. This flower and stem would look good in handstitch or machine embroidery.*

Throughout history, flowers have stimulated us and enhanced and improved our lives. They grace all our important festivals and ceremonies, often figure in the emotional moments in our lives and suffuse our gardens and homes with fragrance and colour. Daisy studded lawns and the lush, herbaceous borders of a country garden packed with Solomon's seal, lady's mantle, China asters, and foxgloves provide a wealth of texture, shape and shade to inspire and delight embroiderers.

Designing with flowers is an enjoyable experience as they so easily lend themselves to a variety of embroidery techniques. The fluttering delicate petals of asters and chrysanthemums translate beautifully into three-dimensional appliqué and can be interpreted in crisp organdies or flimsy chiffons, readily available in a palette of floral colours. Linear details such as leaves and stems can be stitched directly onto a textured background fabric such as velvet, creating a shadowy suggestion. Floral motifs can be scaled down and stylized to use in bonded fabric appliqué. The vibrant colours can then be covered with the use of lush coloured silks. You'll soon find how perfectly embroidery techniques celebrate the contrasting personalities and vitality of flowers.

Right – *Clusters of berry seeds create a regular pattern that could be interpreted by French knots or in reverse appliqué.*
Below – *The subtle colour change offered here would be an interesting starting point for dying fabrics or for bleaching out areas of colour.*

Opposite page: top – *Delicate folds of rose petals are reminiscent of layers of floaty chiffon in a wonderfully contrasting palette. Stitch down lightly to leave edges free;*
below left – *Dramatic form and contrasting colours refresh the eye. Start a new palette in dashing colours and use a flower's shape to consider the possibilities of a daring hat;*
below right – *The way the light strikes the bell-shaped flower head provides a lovely tonal change. This type of flower offers a distinctive design motif.*

Left – A stunning combination of yellow and burnt orange combined in these textured flowers that would work well in machine embroidery and enhanced with hand stitches.
Right – There is a delicate contrast between the centre of these flowers and the floaty ethereal petals that surround them. Stitch using three-dimensional appliqué and chiffon fabric.

Opposite page – A spray of leaves bursting out from a centre stem form a pretty linear type motif that could evolve into a variety of hand or machine stitched projects.

Left – This flower's layered petals and its rich orange colouring beg to be interpreted as an exciting edging in layered and carefully burnt organdie.

Left – The dramatic outline shown here offers an instant motif for repeats as well as outline shapes for objects such as a fun hat or bag.
Right – Creamy pastel rose petals suggest a palette suitable for interpretation as a bridal accessory or dress. Use silk to create a particularly luxurious effect.

Floral Summer Hat

This delicate fabric hat was inspired by a wedding bouquet. I tried to capture the soft colours and the romance of a special occasion. The ruffled appliqué technique is three-dimensional and the hat band can be added to a bought hat – or follow the instructions provided and make a hat to match the colour of a chosen outfit.

Materials and Equipment

- 50cm (20in) gold organdie, 114cm (45in) wide
- 25cm (10in) coral chiffon, 114cm (45in) wide
- 150cm (59in) lilac dupion, 114cm (45in) wide
- 25cm (10in) rose pink dupion, 114cm (45in) wide
- 25cm (10in) sage green dupion, 114cm (45in) wide
- 25cm (10in) silver green dupion, 114cm (45in) wide
- 60 x 114cm (24 x 45in) piece of medium-soft iron-on interfacing
- 60 x 2.5cm (24 x 1in) white petersham waistbanding
- Anchor machine embroidery threads: 1 reel each of candy pink 2346, plum 2565, dusky pink 2383 and old gold 2664
- Machine sewing thread to match lilac dupion
- Hat pattern enlarged to fit from templates on pages 138/139
- Sewing machine
- 18cm (7in) embroidery hoop
- Embroidery scissors
- Tracing paper
- Pencil
- Masking tape
- Iron
- Basic sewing kit (see page 136)

Gerbera with detail

Dahlia

Gerbera (large)

Aster

Leaf

Scroll

Gerbera (medium)

Gerbera (small)

Embroidery

1 Cut two 24cm (9in) squares of gold organdie and lay these together in the embroidery hoop, stretching the fabric tightly.

2 Trace the eight floral templates provided opposite onto a sheet of tracing paper. Most of the fabrics used are transparent and therefore the templates can then be traced off directly onto the fabric using a sharp pencil. Begin by tracing off the large gerbera motif three times onto the gold organdie in the hoop, spacing it economically on the fabric. Then trace off the gerbera with detail twice. Only trace the outlines; centre lines are for stitch guidance only.

3 Set the machine up for free machine embroidery (see page 124) and thread up with candy pink top thread and dusky pink bobbin thread. Practise on a doubled sample of the fabric first to ensure correct tension.

4 Place the hoop into the machine, lower the presser foot lever and embroider around the edge of each motif twice, keeping the stitches

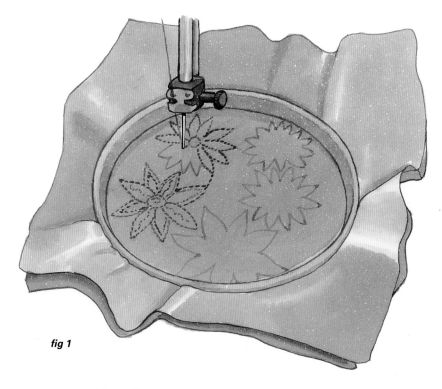

fig 1

small and neat (*fig 1*). Remember, the closer the stitches, the less chance there is of their unravelling once the thread has been trimmed.

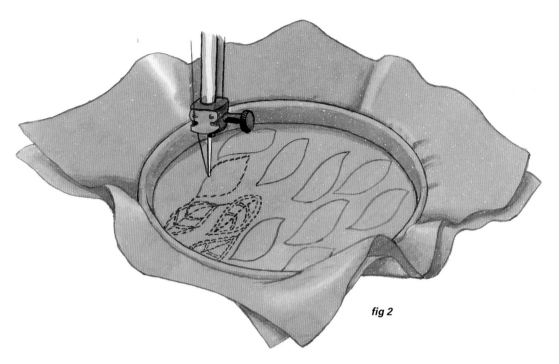

fig 2

5 Carry the thread between two motifs by raising the presser foot lever to disengage the tension, then raising the needle and moving the fabric across. Lower the needle and the presser foot lever and start to sew again.

6 Once all the gold motifs have been stitched, trim away excess threads and carefully cut around each motif.

7 Repeat the above process for the dahlias and asters, but this time placing a 24cm (9in) square of gold organdie over rose pink dupion. Trace off four dahlias and fourteen asters. Thread up the machine with plum top thread and dusky pink bobbin thread.

8 Cut 24cm (9in) squares of coral chiffon and lilac dupion, place together in the hoop and trace and embroider sixteen medium and eight small gerbera as well as eight scrolls. The scrolls are simply outlined. Cut around each.

9 To make the leaves, cut 24cm (9in) squares of sage green dupion and silver green dupion, place together in the hoop and trace off twelve leaves. You may need to use a light box as neither fabric is transparent. (Refer to page 137 for advice on transferring designs.) Thread up the machine with old gold top thread and dusky pink bobbin thread, and embroider the leaves (*fig 2*). Cut around each leaf.

10 Cut a strip of gold organdie 18cm (7in) wide by the length of your hat band. Fold in half lengthways, pin, and stitch the long seam, allowing a 1.5cm (⅝in) seam. Turn right-side out and press so that the seam lies in the middle of the strip, with pressed folds along the top and bottom edge (*fig 3*).

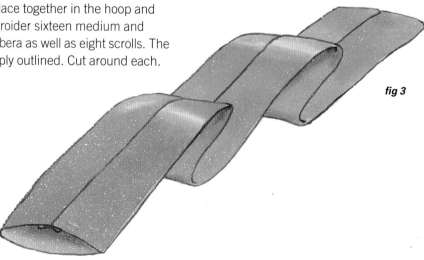

fig 3

fig 4

11 Now spend some time laying all your motifs onto the gold strip. Try different arrangements but always overlap the petals and use the motifs that have two colours together in alternate placings (i.e. pink side up twice, then gold side up twice). This part of the process can take almost as long as the embroidery as the combinations are endless. Do make sure that you leave a 1.5cm (⅝in) seam allowance at either end of the strip.

12 When you are happy with the design, pin and stitch the motifs. Stitch around the centre of each flower and not around the petals (*fig 4*). The leaves and scrolls should be caught at one point only.

13 Once the motifs are attached, run your fingers through them to ruffle them up. Some fraying may take place outside the stitched lines on the flowers; trim these threads away.

fig 1

Hat Construction

1 Follow the instructions given on page 138 to enlarge the hat pattern provided on pages 138/139. Then trace and cut the pattern pieces out of tracing paper. You should have a top, crown and brimpiece.

2 Fold the remaining lilac dupion in half, lay the pattern pieces onto the fabric and cut two of each as shown (*fig 1*).

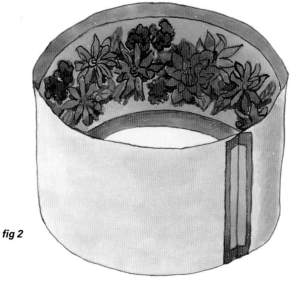

fig 2

3 Cut one top, one crown and two brims from the interfacing and iron them onto the appropriate lilac pieces. You will be left with one crown and one top section unstiffened. These will form the hat's lining.

4 Pin the embroidered floral band to the stiffened lilac crown section, ensuring the long seamed side of the band lies against the right side of the crown. Fold these in half to join the short seams, with the embroidery on the inside, pin and machine stitch (*fig 2*). Use a machine thread that matches the lilac dupion.

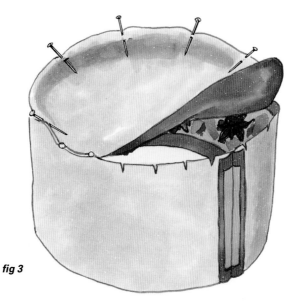

fig 3

5 Pin the stiffened top into the top edge of the stitched crown (*fig 3*). It may take a little time to ease this together; if the top will not sit correctly, clip lightly into the top edge of the crown in order to make it a little wider. Machine stitch in place and remove the pins.

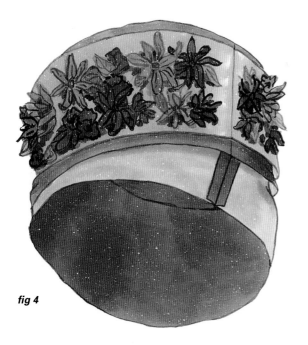

fig 4

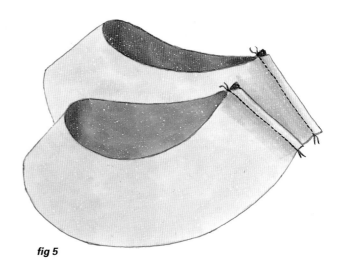

fig 5

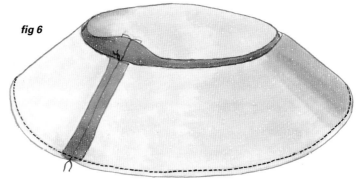

fig 6

6 Now pin and stitch together the unstiffened linings, press all the seams and, turning right side out, place the linings and finished embroidered top wrong sides together (*fig 4*). Edge stitch along the base.

7 Place each brim section short sides together and stitch (*fig 5*), then place the brim sections right sides together and stitch along the outside edge (*fig 6*). Turn the right way out and press under a medium iron.

8 Place the brim over the crown and lining and sew together along the raw edges. Raw edges can be overlocked or zigzag stitched. Push the overlocked edges up towards the inside of the hat, and pin waistbanding in place to cover them (*fig 7*). Hand stitch in place. Fold and overstitch the ends of the waistbanding where they join to prevent fraying.

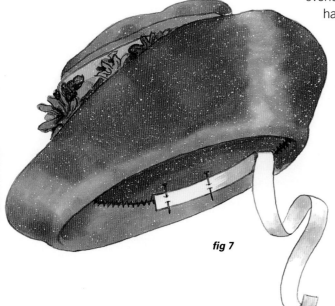

fig 7

Narcissi
Shot Velvet Stole

By using a luxurious shot velvet which has a soft drape and combining it with detailed floral motifs inspired by botanical studies of narcissi, you can create a sumptuous stole which is not only large enough to be practical but is also wonderful to look at.

Materials and Equipment
- 150 x 90cm (59 x 35½in) shot purple/pink velvet
- Machine sewing thread to match velvet
- Anchor machine embroidery threads: 1 reel each of yellow 2110, green 2639 and orange 2285, and Christallina metallic gold 300
- Sewing machine
- 24cm (9in) embroidery hoop
- Embroidery scissors
- Tracing paper
- Pencil
- Basic sewing kit (see page 136)

fig 1

Embroidery

1 Trace the narcissi motif shown below onto four sheets of tracing paper. Note that two will be used with the motif reversed.

Narcissi motif

2 Cut the velvet into two lengths, each 150 x 45cm (59 x 17¾in). Place the traced motifs onto the right side of one length of fabric, positioning two motifs at either end (*fig 1*). Position as you prefer, but keep all motifs the same distance from the edges of the fabric and point the top of each motif towards the stole's centre so that it will look correct when draped around the body. Pin and baste the traced motifs in place.

3 Set your machine for free machine embroidery (see page 124), then thread the top and bobbin with orange thread. Frame one motif in the embroidery hoop and stitch over the pencil lines (*fig 2*). Use one line of stitching for the stems and to outline the flowers. Tear away all the tracing paper when the outline stitching has been done. You should now have the motif stitched directly onto the fabric.

fig 2

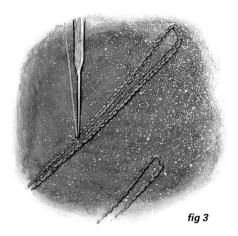

fig 3

4 Begin to stitch into the edges of the petals with the orange thread, using the machine's needle and thread as if it were a coloured pencil and 'sketching' in the details. Use the photographs on page 22 and above as guides.

5 Change the top thread to yellow and stitch the remainder of the petals and the centre of the flower.

6 Use the gold thread in the top to subtly highlight the stamens and the centre lines of the petals. The thread will sink into the velvet pile and will change as the light strikes it.

7 Change the top thread to green and stitch over the stems a few times (*fig 3*), creating a slightly thicker line than the first orange outline. Outline stitch the leaves in green before filling in with long rows of stitches. Try to stitch smoothly along the length.

8 Trim off all surface thread ends before removing the velvet from the hoop. If the hoop leaves slight marks on the velvet pile, hold the fabric over the steam from a kettle to raise the pile again.

9 Repeat steps 3–8 to complete the three remaining motifs.

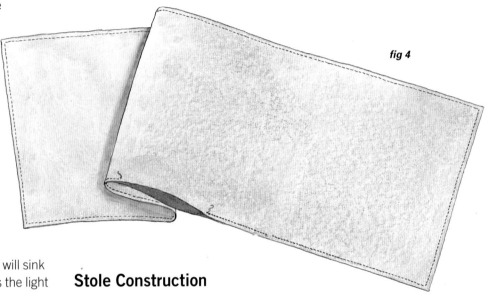

fig 4

Stole Construction

1 Set the machine for straight stitch and attach the normal presser foot. Use a machine thread to match the velvet.

2 Place the embroidered velvet length and the plain velvet length right sides together, pin and baste, leaving a 1.5cm (⅝in) seam allowance. Mark a 15cm (6in) opening in one of the long side seams and machine stitch all round, finishing at the other end of the opening (*fig 4*).

3 Clip excess fabric away from the corners, but take care not to snip the stitching line (*fig 5*).

4 Turn the stole the right way out, pushing out the corners neatly, then slip stitch the opening to finish. Press lightly around the seams if necessary, using the point of an iron. If the pile has been slightly flattened, sprinkle lightly with water then place the stole in a tumble dryer for a maximum of 30 seconds.

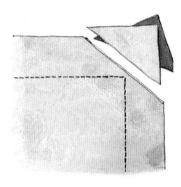

fig 5

Bouquet Brooches

These brooches are quick to make and form charming gifts.
The colours could be customized to fit with a favourite outfit.
They use only tiny amounts of fabric and are therefore ideal for
using up the leftover scraps from other projects. They could also
be made up without pins for creating pictures or cards.

Materials and Equipment
- Medium-weight calico large
  enough to fit into hoop
- Scraps of fabric in the following
  colours: gold, pale pink, lilac,
  orange, white, green
- Leather or vinyl (for backing
  brooches)
- Iron-on interfacing (scraps)
- Fusible fabric bond (enough to
  back scraps)
- Anchor machine embroidery
  threads: 1 reel each of bronze
  2761 and orange 2285
- Sewing machine
- Small embroidery hoop
- Embroidery scissors
- Contact cement glue
- Fray check fabric edging or
  PVA glue
- 2.5cm (1in) brooch pins
- Fine paintbrush
- Pencil
- Iron
- Basic sewing kit (see page 136)

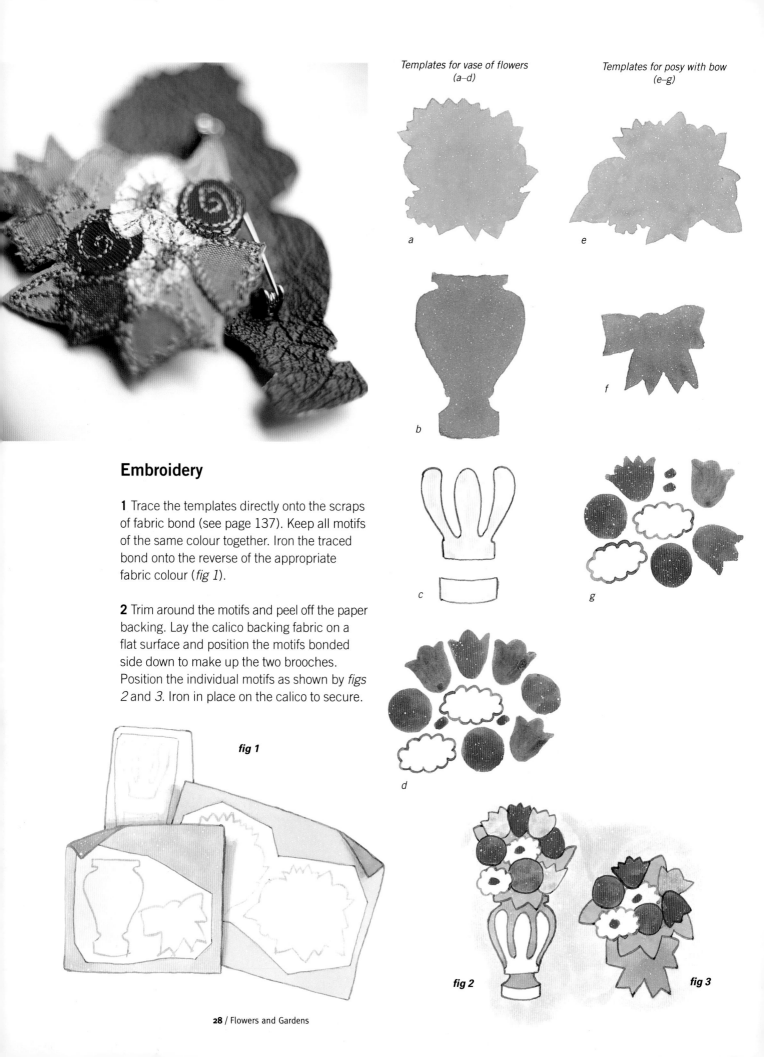

Templates for vase of flowers (a–d)

a

b

c

Templates for posy with bow (e–g)

e

f

g

d

Embroidery

1 Trace the templates directly onto the scraps of fabric bond (see page 137). Keep all motifs of the same colour together. Iron the traced bond onto the reverse of the appropriate fabric colour (*fig 1*).

2 Trim around the motifs and peel off the paper backing. Lay the calico backing fabric on a flat surface and position the motifs bonded side down to make up the two brooches. Position the individual motifs as shown by *figs 2* and *3*. Iron in place on the calico to secure.

fig 1

fig 2

fig 3

3 Place the calico in the embroidery hoop, making sure the fabric is taut. Then set your machine for free machine embroidery (see page 124).

4 Thread up the machine with bronze top thread and orange bobbin thread. Keeping the stitches small, carefully outline the vase, bow and the two bouquets twice (*fig 4*).

5 Fill in the white daisy shapes with petals, then fill in the pink roses with spirals. Embroider around the orange and lilac tulips. On the posy brooch, stitch a vein line onto each leaf. Finally, fill in the vase with spiral stitching.

6 Trim away excess threads and iron carefully.

7 Iron a piece of interfacing onto the reverse of the stitched brooches. This prevents glue from the vinyl or leather backing seeping through. Then neatly trim around each brooch (*fig 5*).

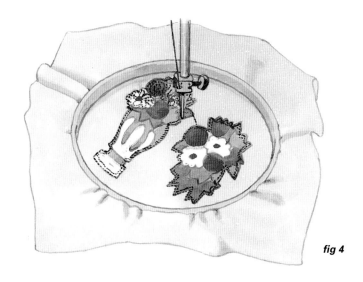

fig 4

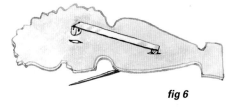

fig 5

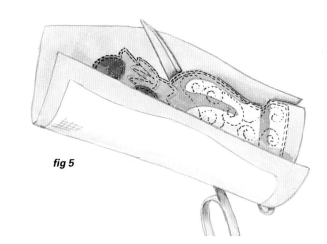

fig 6

8 Use the stitched piece as a guide to cut a vinyl or leather backing, cutting it slightly bigger than the stitched piece. Make two small cuts in the backing fabric and press the pin and hook of the brooch through. This ensures that the brooch length is hidden behind the backing (*fig 6*).

9 Spread contact cement glue onto the reverse of each brooch and its backing and allow to 'cure' for as long as the manufacturer recommends. Press each brooch and backing together firmly and allow to dry.

10 Carefully trim away excess vinyl, then paint the edges with a fray check product or PVA glue to seal.

city and
architecture

Above: *Simple, carved stone inspired motifs
are wonderful for appliqué techniques.*
Opposite page: top left – *Pillars provide an
ideal framework for all kinds of imagery.
Cut away the centres to create transparent
effects as in cutwork;*
top right – *Water soluble embroidery is ideal
for interpreting the curvilinear structures
commonly found in wrought-iron work;*
below left – *The geometry of these curves
and angles should inspire a Hardanger
project enhanced with couched thread;*
below right – *Lichen and moss offer a
natural colour foil to the cool grey of worn
stonework. Interpret the stone in slate satin
enhanced with hand dyed silk threads.*

Every built-up environment provides
distinct imagery, ranging from strong
geometrics to light and shade passing
through windows, that is perfect to
translate and utilize for stitch projects.

It is easy to overlook our immediate surroundings as a source of inspiration, but there is an enormous variety of design sources within any town or city. I was brought up in a country town, but when I moved to Glasgow, Scotland, to study art I fell in love with the city's Victorian architecture and it has inspired much of my work. The decorative plasterwork, the rich colours and the attention to detail inside and out still fascinates me today. Even modern high-rise structures provide shape, depth and repeat patterns that can form the beginnings of an interesting and workable design. Alternatively, simple marks taken from rubbings of stone walls are a good starting point for translating hand stitches into textures. Rusty corrugated metal is challenging to draw and translate for design purposes, but it suggests a variety of machine and hand stitch techniques and provides a wonderful palette as an inspiration for dyeing fabrics. From small scale texture to grand scale opulence it is not difficult to find an aspect of architecture to appeal to even the novice designer/embroiderer.

In the three projects that follow, inspiration was sourced from the intricacies of wrought-iron work, the strength of texture within stone carving and the graceful structure of pillars and archways, each suggesting a specific technique, including Hardanger and machine appliqué.

Right – *Iron-work has been stylized into a leaf shape that would work as an embroidered appliqué motif.*
Below – *Curving wrought iron is ideal source material for using with a technique such as couching or whipping stitch.*

Opposite page: top – *Decorative stonework in soft hues could be considered for ornate interpretations in machine embroidery or as a freestyle hand-stitched original;*
below left – *Consider the possibilities of a design inspired by bricks, especially when laid out in a format such as this kite-shaped arrangement;*
below right – *The composition of these railings would evolve easily into a border repeat for a soft furnishings collection or jewellery pieces in water soluble techniques.*

Left – A stained-glass panel suggests reverse appliqué techniques – perhaps enhanced with couching.
Right – This pretty but crumbling pillar decorated with a swag of carved flowers lends itself to a myriad of machine or hand-stitched techniques.

Opposite page – The shadowy glimpse of colour and form seen through the wrought-iron gate suggests layering up floaty voile fabrics and decorating the surface with couched metallic cords.

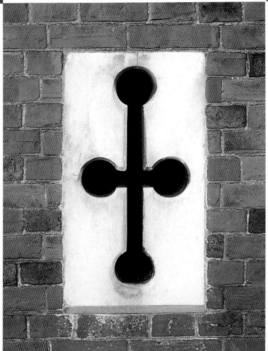

Left – This protective battlement window in the shape of a cross is bold and distinctive. It would translate well if used in a cross stitch or tent stitch design.

Left – Arch shapes are popular for use in all sorts of design projects. This one's clean outlines would work well in a crisp linen. The soft stonework colours make a sophisticated palette.
Right – An image such as these rusted metal spikes evokes thoughts of structured edges or of tassels made from shiny threads.

Appliquéd Pillar Window Covering

The combination of crumbling pillars and linking archways from an Italian garden is appealing as an inspiration for design. Look at the contrasts between the strong stone structures and the way light comes flooding through the archways.

  The transparent voile and organza fabric layer used in this project allows light to fill a room, but the detailed band of the embroidery at the base provides a focus and structure to the piece. The technique is a combination of appliqué and shadow work. This project can be adapted to fit any window.

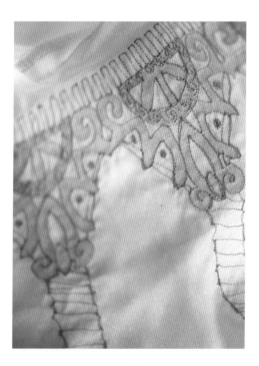

Materials and Equipment
- 2.5m (2¾yds) cotton voile, 114cm (45in) wide
- 2.5m (2¾yds) cotton organza, 114cm (45in) wide (or to fit length and width of chosen window)
- 35cm (14in) cream dupion silk, 114cm (45in) wide
- 15cm (6in) silver grey dupion silk, 114cm (45in) wide
- 50 x 114cm (20 x 45in) iron-on fabric bond
- Anchor machine embroidery threads: 1 reel each of stone 2838 and silver grey 2512
- Sewing machine
- 24cm (9in) embroidery hoop
- Embroidery scissors
- Tracing paper
- Set square
- Pencil
- Iron
- Basic sewing kit (see page 136)

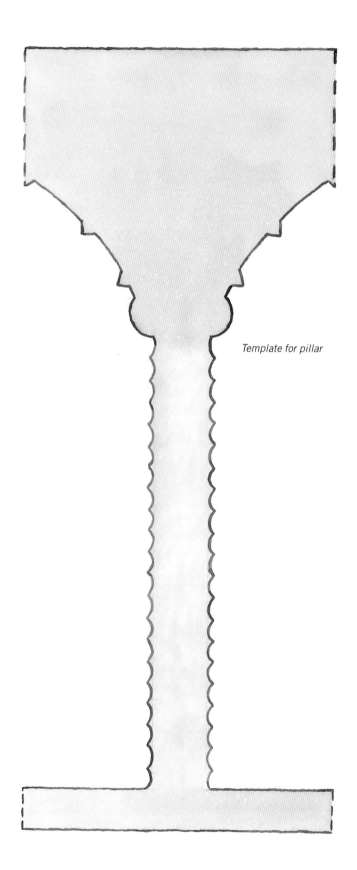

Template for pillar

Template for pillar detail

Embroidery

1 Trim 30cm (12in) from the lengths of both the organza and the voile and leave to one side. This fabric will form five tab tops to hold the window covering on the curtain pole. Now measure 30cm (12in) from the lower edge of the remaining length of voile and mark a fold across the width with an iron. Unfold (*fig 1*). The pressed line will be used as a placing guide for the base of the pillar templates.

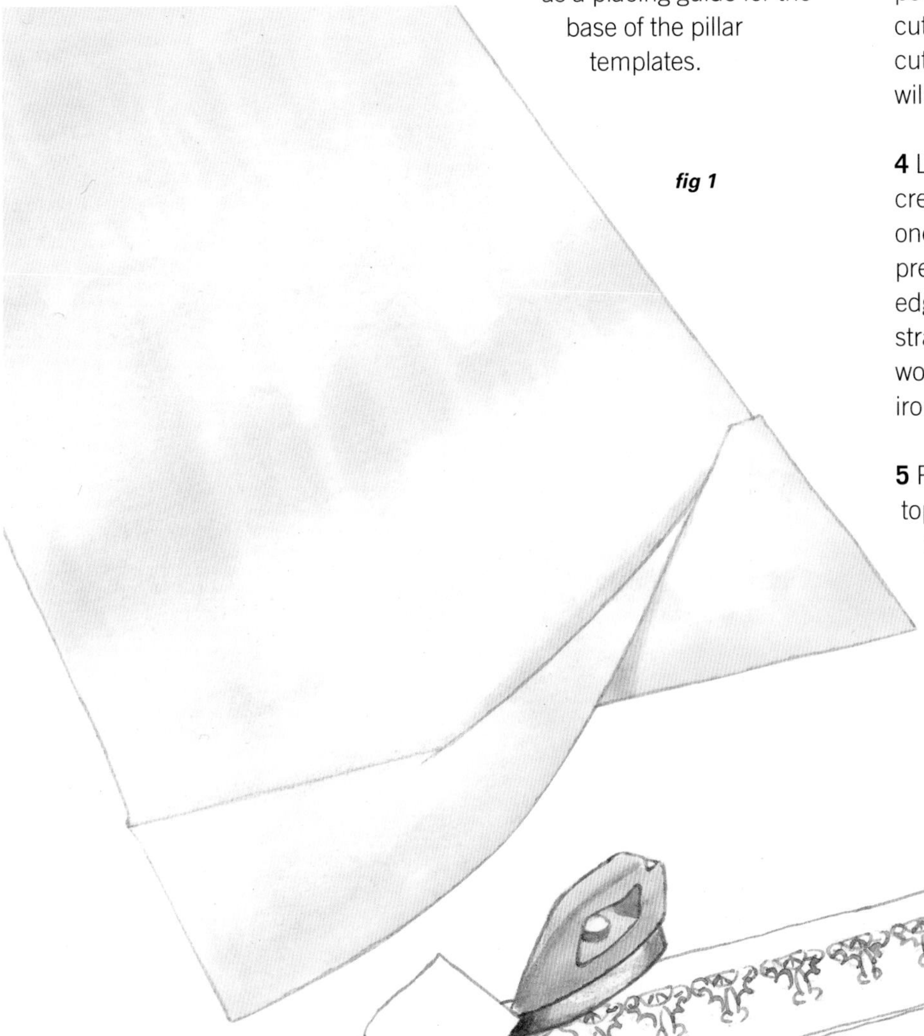

fig 1

2 Cut a 35cm (14in) width of fabric bond and trace ten pillar templates onto this, linking the shapes at the top and bottom. On the remaining fabric bond trace off ten pillar detail templates, again linking the shapes. Iron the pillars onto the reverse of the cream dupion and the details onto the reverse of the silver grey dupion (*fig 2*).

3 Cut around each template carefully, then peel off the paper backing. You may be able to cut the shapes to link at top and bottom, but cut them individually if you prefer; the joins will not show on the finished project.

4 Lay the voile on a flat surface and line up the cream pillar motifs. Begin 7cm (2¾in) in from one edge to allow for a seam and use the pressed line as a guide to align the bottom edge of the pillars. Ensure the pillars are straight both horizontally and vertically: it's worth checking with a set square before ironing them in place.

5 Position the silver grey detail motifs at the top of each pillar, then iron in place. Press firmly to bond on top of the cream dupion.

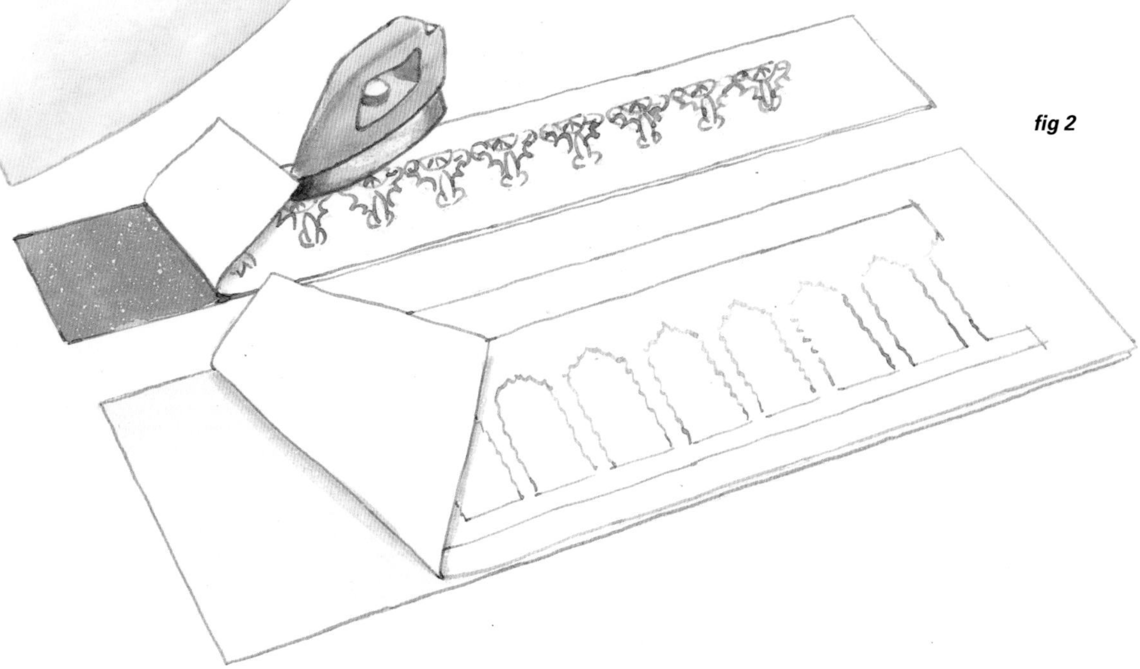

fig 2

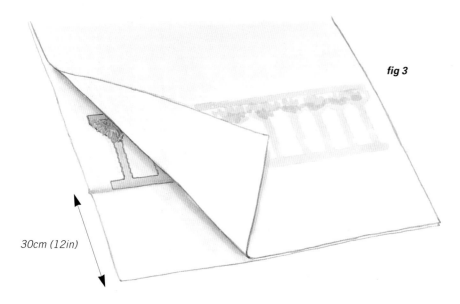

fig 3

30cm (12in)

sewing a small tight spiral outwards to the desired size. Then fill in the carved half circle with spirals. Embroider the diagonal lines on each pillar before you outline the pillars.

9 Embroider all the motifs before stitching the top and bottom bands – these are easier left till last. Try to get as much of the band in the embroidery hoop at any one time in order to keep the lines as continuous and smooth as possible.

10 On completion, remove the fabric from the hoop and press the covering lightly with an iron on the reverse. Neaten up by trimming away any surface threads. Or pull all loose threads through to the reverse, knot and trim.

6 Lay the organza fabric on top of the voile, sandwiching the bonded motifs in-between (*fig 3*). Baste around the edge of the fabric layers and baste a few rows horizontally and vertically to keep the layers flat while working.

7 Set the machine up for free machine embroidery (see page 124), with stone top thread and silver grey bobbin thread. Then place one motif in the embroidery hoop and begin by outlining the carved plaster details, referring to the stitch diagram (*fig 4*). Try to sew in a continuous line, but where this is not possible lift the presser lever and raise the needle before moving the fabric. Keep the stitches small and trim away surface threads.

8 Continue by embroidering the dots on the plaster detail by starting in the centre and

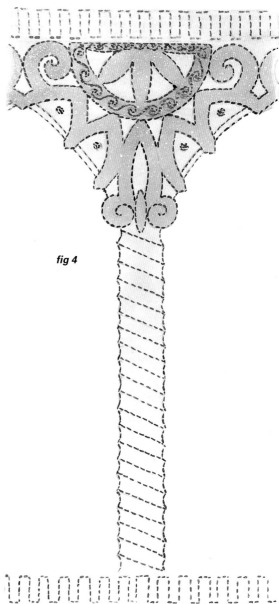

fig 4

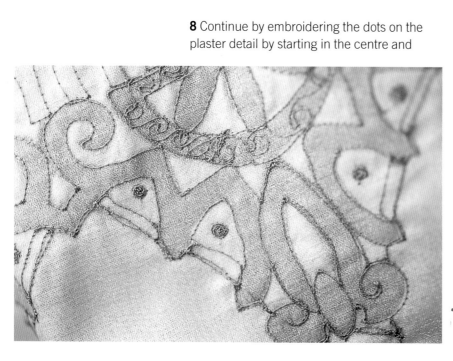

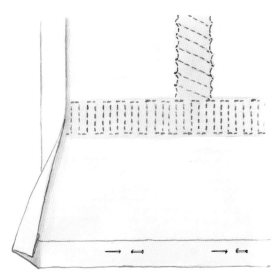

fig 5

Curtain Construction

1 Cut away excess width at each side of the motifs up the long edge of the fabric to leave a 3.5cm (1⅜in) seam allowance. Pin the raw edges under by 1cm (⅜in) all round. Then fold the edges under again by 1.5cm (⅝in), re-pinning and basting in place (*fig 5*). Iron lightly to create a crisp fold. Finish the top and bottom edge in the same way

2 Set the machine up for straight stitch and replace the presser foot before stitching the seams.

3 Place together the organza and voile fabric strips that you saved for tab tops at the start of the project and cut out five double layers, each measuring 30 x 12cm (12 x 4¾in). Fold each doubled fabric tab lengthways, organza sides together, then pin and stitch the seam (*fig 6*). Reverse stitch at the start and finish of each seam to prevent it from unravelling.

4 Turn the tubes of fabric the right way out and press with the seam centred (*fig 7*).

5 Fold the tubes in half, bringing the long seams together, and pin under the raw edges before placing them onto the reverse of the top edge of the window covering. Space the tabs evenly, then pin and stitch in place. Remove all pins and basting stitches. They should now slide onto most curtain poles. Extra tabs can be added if you choose to make wider curtains.

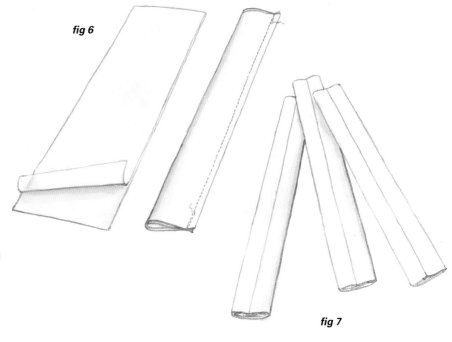

fig 6

fig 7

Renaissance Hair Clasps

The intricate plasterwork details found on many classical buildings can be translated into a variety of motifs suitable for use in embroidery. By breaking the carvings down into simple elements then recreating them with an appliqué technique the final result looks very intricate. A small project such as this hair clasp is ideal for beginners in clearly demonstrating how a design can be built up from a familiar object. You could work all sorts of colour combinations to match different outfits.

Materials and Equipment

- Calico backing fabric large enough to fit into hoop
- Scraps of silk in 'stone' shades as follows: light gold, mid-brown/pink, dark brown
- Leather or vinyl (for backing clasps)
- Iron-on interfacing (scraps)
- Fusible fabric bond (scraps)
- Anchor machine embroidery threads: 1 reel each of gold 2724 and bronze 2761
- Sewing machine
- Small embroidery hoop
- Embroidery scissors
- Contact cement glue
- Hair clip (available from craft shops and bead suppliers)
- Pencil
- Iron
- Basic sewing kit (see page 136)

Template a
Cut one in dark brown

Template b
Cut two in light gold

Template c
Cut two in mid-brown/pink

Template d
Cut one in mid-brown/pink

Template e
Cut one in mid-brown/pink

fig 1

Embroidery

1 Trace the templates given onto the paper backing of the fabric bond, spacing them economically and tracing the quantities required for each colour.

2 Iron *template a* onto the reverse of the dark brown silk, *template b* onto the reverse of the light gold silk (note this involves two templates) and the remaining templates onto the mid-brown/pink silk.

3 Use small embroidery scissors to cut around the templates carefully (*fig 1*). Then peel off the paper backing.

4 Lay the calico backing fabric on a flat surface and iron *template a* onto it. Lay the remainder of the templates on top of *template a*, positioning as shown by *fig 2*. Iron to bond in place.

5 Stretch the fabric in the hoop and set the machine for free machine embroidery (see page 124). Thread up with gold thread in the bobbin and bronze thread on the top.

6 Embroider all around shapes *b–e* then fill in the detail lines on *templates b–d*. Start at the centre of the spiral for the scrolls on *template b* and work outwards. For *templates c–d*, stitch just within the edge of each shape before stitching the inner details. Keep the stitches as small as possible to prevent the thread from unravelling. Trim all thread ends and remove fabric from the hoop. Iron carefully.

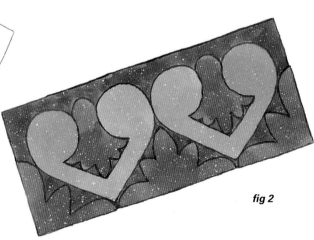

fig 2

7 Set the machine back to normal by raising the feed dog and using a zigzag foot. Set the machine for satin stitch (width 4). Thread up the top and the bobbin with gold. Then, begining with one long edge, carefully sew around the edge of the clasp design. Finish this long edge 4mm (⅛in) from the end, lift the presser foot and turn the clasp around ready to stitch the short edge, making sure you start the first stitch at the very edge (*fig 3*). Continue all around then pull all thread ends through to the reverse and knot.

8 Iron interfacing onto the reverse of the embroidery to strengthen it before trimming around the clasp with sharp scissors. Trim as close to the satin stitch as possible, but take care not to cut any stitches.

9 Cut a piece of leather or vinyl backing slightly larger than the clasp. Spread glue over the wrong side of the backing and the wrong side of the clasp, then leave to 'cure' according to the manufacturer's instructions before pressing the clasp and backing together.

10 Once the glue has dried, trim off excess vinyl before gluing a hair clip onto the back.

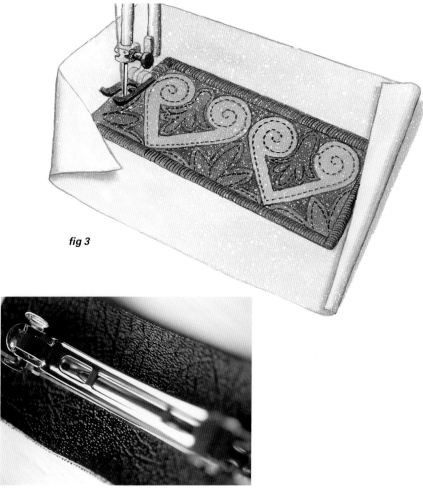

fig 3

Hardanger
Wrought-Iron Cushion

The technique of Hardanger originated in Norway. It is made up of blocks of stitchwork with cutwork centres, which for this project I found a little reminiscent of bricks and windows. As a contrast to the geometric style, I have added detailing which was inspired by wrought iron and then finished the cushion with a decorative metallic cord.

Materials and Equipment

- 40cm (16in) square of white 22-count Hardanger fabric
- 38cm (15in) square of white lining fabric
- 38cm (15in) square of white backing fabric
- 10g ball of white pearl cotton, No. 5
- 10g ball of white pearl cotton, No. 8
- 1 skein of fine metallic cord for couching
- 24cm (9in) embroidery hoop
- Tapestry needles, No. 20 & 24
- Embroidery scissors
- 35cm (14in) square cushion pad
- 2m (2¼yd) length of metallic cord (optional)
- Basic sewing kit (see page 136)

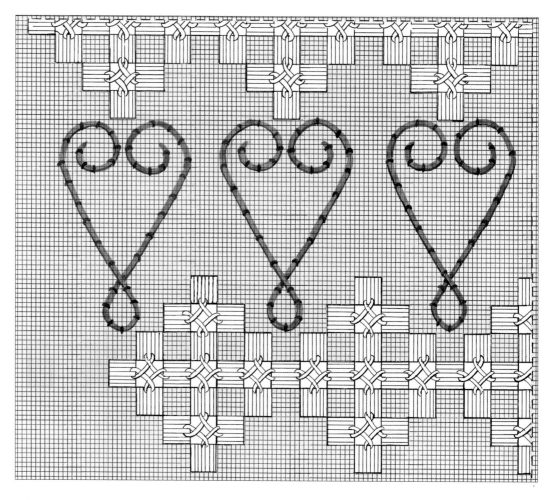

Embroidery

1 Fold the Hardanger fabric in half lengthways and widthways to find the centre point, then baste the centre lines (*fig 1*). Only the lower half of the chart is shown: it mirrors upwards for the full design. Match the top edge of the chart with the horizontal basting line. The vertical basting line should match the vertical dashed line on the chart.

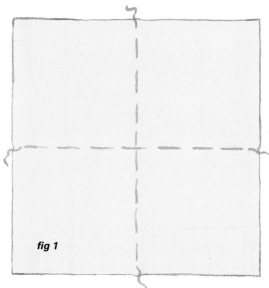

fig 1

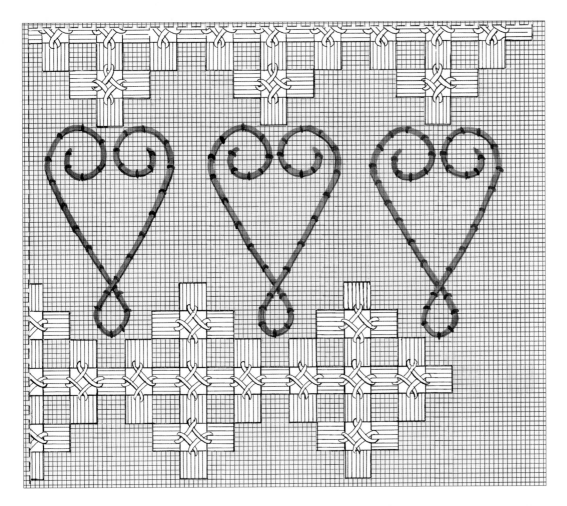

2 Tension the fabric in the embroidery hoop and, using a No. 20 tapestry needle threaded with pearl cotton (No. 5), sew the first satin stitch block (see page 122) over the centre point. Follow the chart to complete all the blocks, mirroring the chart to complete the top half of the cushion. Remember to sew tails under the reverse of the stitches to secure.

3 When you have finished the blocks, use small embroidery scissors to trim away alternate block centres within the design. Cut centres are represented on the chart by blank areas.

4 The cut centres are filled in with dove's eye filling (see page 122), using a No. 24 tapestry needle threaded with pearl cotton (No. 8).

5 Thread a No. 20 needle with the fine metallic cord and add the wrought-iron detailing, using a couching technique (see page 119).

6 Trim the embroidered fabric to a 38cm (15in) square. Then pin and baste the white lining to the wrong side of the embroidered fabric.

7 Now pin the backing fabric and the embroidered fabric right sides together, baste and machine stitch, allowing a 1.5cm (⅝in) seam. Trim away the corner points and turn right side out.

8 Place a cushion pad inside and slip stitch the open side to finish. Trim with decorative metallic cord if desired, twisting the cord to form a loop at each corner.

sea and sky

The breadth and depth of the ocean meets the clear blue of the sky and allows a variety of living forms to thrive. The environment offers endless design possibilities for the embroiderer.

The ocean can be very evocative: it is calm or intense and, depending on the geography, the colour varies from an uplifting clear blue to a murky, forbidding indigo. I have memories of favourite holidays spent visiting family friends who lived on an island off the Scottish coast. An added thrill was always the preceding boat trip – it was mesmerizing to look over the boat's rails into the depths of the waves and gaze out to the horizon or to the receding coastline.

Stand on the shore of a beach and you'll see lovely bands of colour, shading from the golden sands beneath your feet to the mid-blue of the ocean and the paler bright blue of the sky. The white froth created by waves rolling onto the shore adds yet more stripes of colour. As a design source it has stunning proportions that make it easy to translate into an idea for embroidery. Look also into rock pools: sea creatures, barnacles and seaweed supply a variety of colour, shape and texture and beg the use of motif and water-soluble fabric embroidery and the use of translucent materials. Try to visit harbours and maritime museums in order to sketch traditional nautical implements that combine form and function. And don't forget holiday photographs and postcards – they provide a never-ending source of images that can be utilized for a sea-theme project.

Right – *Lit by a setting sun, the dusk sky is always breathtaking. Look for unusual colours to translate into embroidery – and interpret them as large shaded stripes.*
Below – *Pearlescent fabrics would be put to clever use in interpreting delicate nautilus shells or any well polished shell.*

Opposite page: top – *A classic piece of imagery in all forms of design is the starfish. It is beautiful, elegant and richly textured and lends itself to interpretation in a variety of projects;*
below left – *This shot of polished pebbles would look crisp and bold as a satin stitch appliqué panel in natural fabrics and colours;*
below right – *Crumbling, fragile and incredibly textural, driftwood could be recreated as a sumptuous embellished velvet or in layered and burnt edge appliqué.*

Left – The rusty links of an anchor chain offer an unusual colour palette but they could be interpreted in chain stitch or in free machine embroidery.
Right – The natural lines etched by the sea and sand in driftwood make wonderfully delicate structures that work when used to inspire textural embroidery.

Opposite page – Coral is visually stimulating in its many forms. This photograph could be translated into an opulent appliqué and machine embroidery design.

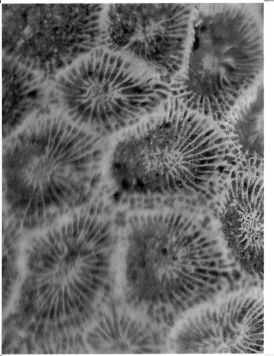

Left – Magnified coral takes on a new perspective with fine tendrils creeping from centre stems. An interesting all-over pattern could be created using free machine stitches.

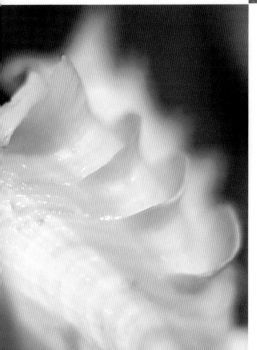

Left – The spines on this pearl shell form a defence but the basic structure looks like pintucks or three-dimensional appliqué.
Right – Jumbled ropes of different textures, colours and widths form an interesting random design. This effect would be ideal for representation in couchwork.

Nautical Tablecloth

The symbols of a nautical life are all included in this project.
A ship's wheel, lifebelt, anchor and ropes are used in a fresh
palette on a linen background. The motifs can be repeated to
make either a table centre or a border around a larger cloth.

Materials and Equipment

- 86cm (34in) square of white linen
- Anchor machine embroidery threads: 1 reel each of yellow 2110, red 2345, royal blue 2548 and black 2012
- White sewing thread
- Sewing machine
- 24cm (9in) embroidery hoop
- Embroidery scissors
- Tracing paper
- Pencil
- Black waterproof pen
- Light box (optional)
- Masking tape
- Iron
- Basic sewing kit (see page 136)

Template for nautical tablecloth

Embroidery

1 Fold and baste the linen fabric with guidelines, running horizontally, vertically and diagonally across its centre point (*fig 1*).

2 Trace the template onto tracing paper using a black waterproof pen. Include all guidelines.

3 The template gives mirror repeats from the centre wheel and, at the other end, mirror repeats from the anchor. It is helpful to have photocopies of the reverse of the tracing in order to plan the overall design (see *fig 2*/page 60).

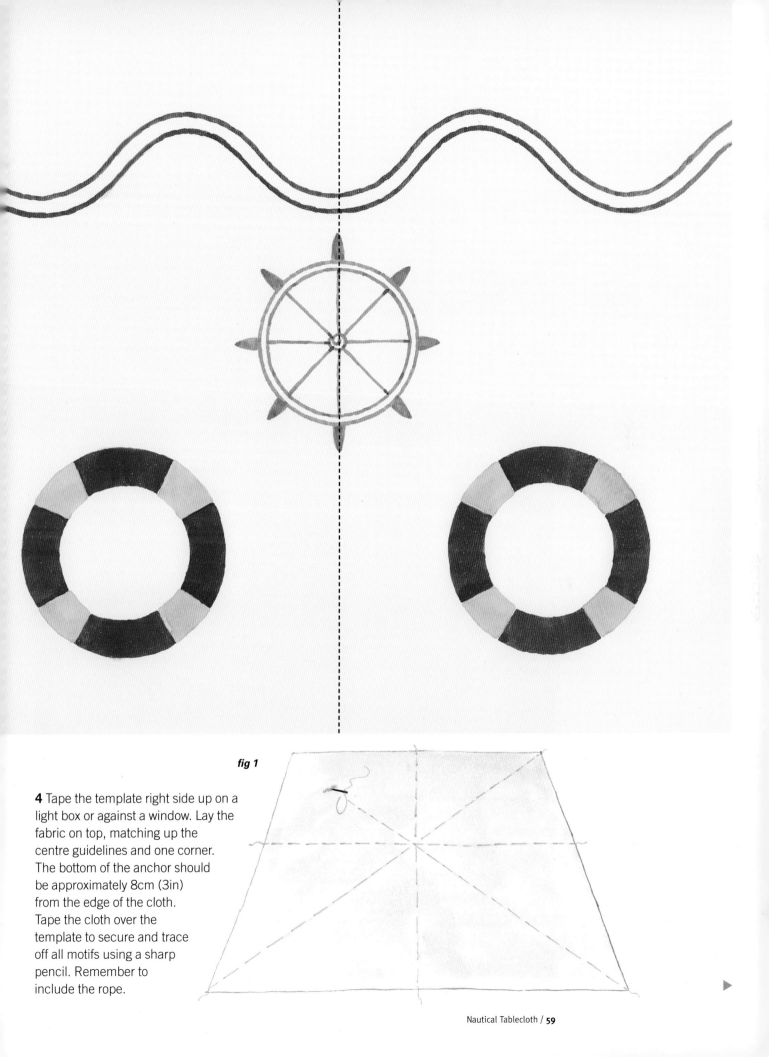

fig 1

4 Tape the template right side up on a light box or against a window. Lay the fabric on top, matching up the centre guidelines and one corner. The bottom of the anchor should be approximately 8cm (3in) from the edge of the cloth. Tape the cloth over the template to secure and trace off all motifs using a sharp pencil. Remember to include the rope.

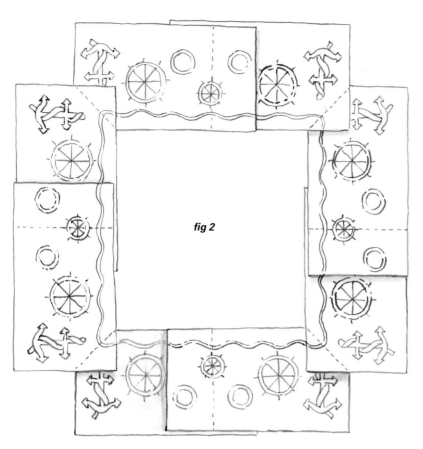

fig 2

5 Reverse the template to turn the corner, reposition the fabric, and continue to trace off the motifs. Continue in this way until the border design is formed.

6 Set the machine for free machine embroidery (see page 124) and thread up with red in the bobbin and on top. Position the fabric in the embroidery hoop and begin by outlining the anchor, keeping the stitches small. Outline stitch all the motifs twice, but do not stitch the rope at this stage.

7 Refer to the coloured template on pages 58/59 and to the photographs to stitch the red motifs. Include the filled-in sections of the lifebelt. The solid areas of colour are created by stitching back and forth in small rows, rather like colouring in with a pencil.

8 Change the bobbin and top thread to yellow and work the yellow motifs. Change the threads again to work the royal blue shapes. Finally, add the black wavy detail to the lifebelt (*fig 3*).

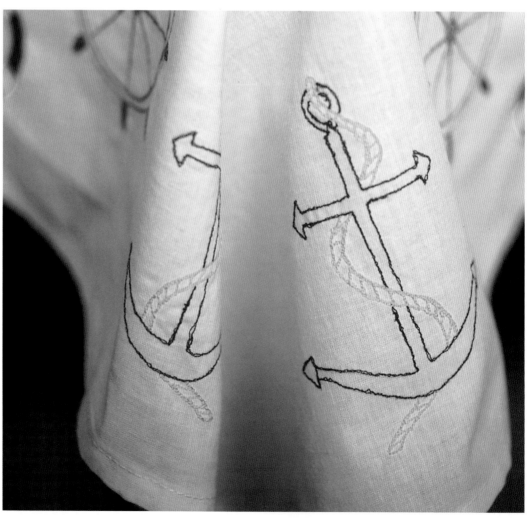

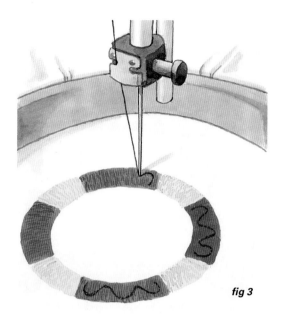

fig 3

9 Outline the rope before adding the twist detail. Try to keep the outlines smooth, especially when you have to reposition the fabric within the hoop. The twist detail is added by working diagonally between the rope's outlines, then stitching along the outline.

Tablecloth Construction

1 To make up the tablecloth, trim all excess threads on the surface and the reverse. The tight stitching means the threads will not continue to unravel.

2 Press the cloth lightly before pinning all the raw edges under by 1cm (⅜in). Fold the edges under again by 1.5cm (⅝in), re-pinning as you go, then press and baste.

3 Set the machine for straight stitch and replace the presser foot. Machine sew the tablecloth's seam.

4 Press to finish.

Marine Greetings Cards

Endless design opportunities are provided by sea-related motifs, with very pretty results. This project uses up leftover fabrics and threads and is ideal for cards, gift tags or framed pictures. The project also provides an introduction to stitching on paper, water soluble embroidery and machine shadow work.

Materials and Equipment
- 1 square of hot water soluble fabric (enough to fit hoop)
- 2 squares of white organdie (enough to fit hoop)
- Scraps of Indian handmade papers (assorted colours)
- Assorted metallic machine embroidery threads
- Scraps of coloured fabrics including gold organdie
- Blank greetings cards and envelopes
- Sewing machine
- Small embroidery hoop
- Embroidery scissors
- PVA glue
- Small candle
- Gold paint (acrylic or gouache)
- Fine paintbrush
- Polystyrene tray
- Basic sewing kit (see page 136)

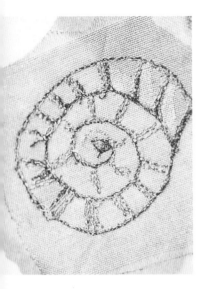

Nautilus Shell

1 Glue two torn squares of paper directly onto a greetings card. Cut a square of gold organdie slightly smaller than the torn papers and carefully burn the edges to create a wavy line. Work over a sink in case of accidents. Then glue this onto the torn paper squares at an angle. Leave to dry.

2 Set the machine for free machine embroidery (see page 124) and use a metallic thread on the top and bottom to stitch a nautilus shell directly onto the card. Keep the stitches close together. Change the thread colour before embroidering the shell's outline (*fig 1*).

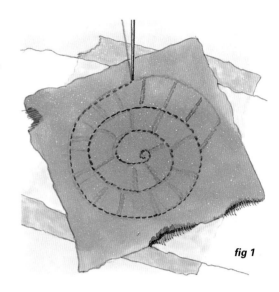

fig 1

Triple Starfish

1 Glue a rectangular strip of torn paper, measuring 3 x 12cm (1¼ x 5in), onto a card. Now tear four thin strips from a contrasting coloured paper, each slightly wider than the original strip. Glue the strips at evenly spaced intervals onto the background paper (*fig 2*). Allow at least 3cm (1¼in) between the strips.

2 Place a piece of organdie on the hoop. Cut tiny scraps of coloured fabric and scatter these over the organdie, ensuring they overlap. Lay a second layer of organdie over the top and fix the hoop's inner frame (*fig 3*). Tension the fabric.

3 Outline machine stitch three simple starfish motifs freehand, spacing them evenly and sizing them so you will be able to trim them to 2cm (¾in) squares. Do not cut until you have embroidered a large scroll starfish and two nautilus shells if you are also making these cards. Then trim the three starfish shapes into squares and glue them into the spaces between the thin strips of paper.

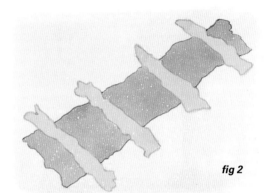

fig 2

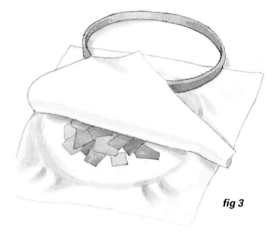

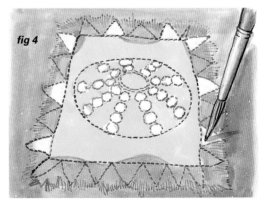

fig 3

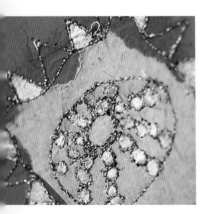

Sea Urchin

1 Glue a double layer of torn paper onto a greetings card, making sure the upper square is slightly smaller than the background square. Machine embroider a sea urchin directly onto the card, then embroider a triangular border. Trim the threads.

2 Use a fine paintbrush and gold paint to highlight the 'spikes' on the urchin and to paint in each alternate border triangle (*fig 4*).

fig 4

Scroll Starfish

Using the same framed fabric as for the triple starfish, free machine embroider one large starfish outline, filling in the centre with scrolls. Embroider a square frame around the starfish and decorate the area immediately around this with scrolls. Trim around the edge of the scrolls before gluing the motif onto a greetings card.

Nautilus Shells

Free machine embroider two nautilus shells as for the scroll starfish but trim and glue onto a double layer of torn papers that you have arranged on a greetings card.

Lacy Starfish

1 Frame the water soluble fabric in the hoop and free machine embroider a starfish motif outline with gold metallic thread. Fill in the motif with lots of linking stitches. The stitches all have to overlap – otherwise the design will fall apart when the fabric dissolves (*fig 5*). This may take a few attempts to get right.

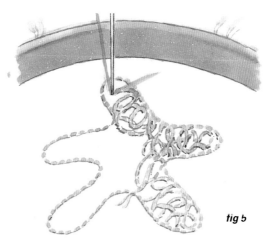

fig 5

2 Trim away any excess water soluble fabric and pin the motif onto a polystyrene tray if possible. Place into a bowl and pour boiling hot water over the motif (*fig 6*). This will dissolve the fabric but leave the embroidery intact. Repeat as necessary, but note that the embroidery may contract a little. Pin the embroidery onto an ironing board and iron dry.

3 Glue a triple layer of handmade papers onto a greetings card and glue the starfish motif to this. Allow to dry, then place in the sewing machine. Remove the thread from the needle and stitch a decorative pattern all around the border, through the layers of handmade paper. This creates a lacy, punched effect in keeping with the lace-effect embroidery.

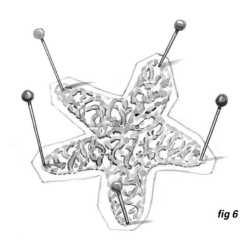

fig 6

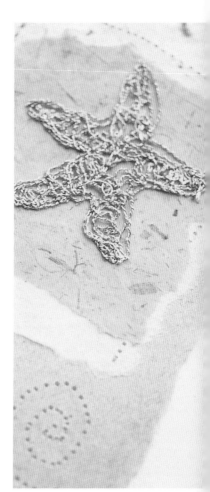

GENERAL TIPS

- It is best to 'draw' the motif as you stitch in order to create a free feel to these cards. There is no need to transfer the designs onto fabric first.

- Stitch as many motifs as you can for each technique in order to build up a stock of cards.

- Change the colours of the trapped fabrics to create a different look each time.

- It is worth practising with the water soluble fabric as much as possible. The final results can be slightly unpredictable.

Seascape Wrap

The idea for this wrap came after a day at the beach, watching the deep cyan of the ocean giving way to the rolling, white-topped waves lapping the shore. Interesting ripples were left in the sand and I've tried to recreate the textures and atmosphere of the day in the wrap. Details such as the starfish and shell beads were added to complete the marine feel.

Materials and Equipment
- 130 x 114cm (51 x 45in) piece of gold dupion
- 25 x 114cm (10 x 45in) piece of pale blue dupion
- 25 x 114cm (10 x 45in) piece of blue organdie
- 50 x 114cm (20 x 45in) piece of gold metallic organza
- 25 x 48cm (10 x 19in) piece of coral organza
- Anchor machine embroidery threads: 1 reel each of pale blue 2521, and Christallina metallic turquoise 321, metallic blue 320, and metallic gold 300
- Machine sewing thread to match gold dupion
- Sewing machine
- Twin needle
- Embroidery scissors
- Small candle
- Ten assorted gold shell beads (optional)
- Iron
- Basic sewing kit (see page 136)

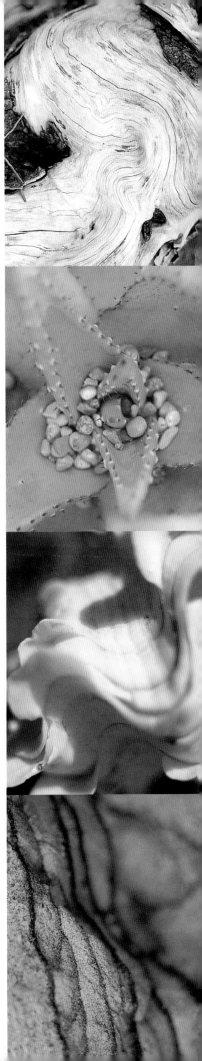

fig 1

gold pleats   coral ripples

Embroidery

1 Cut a piece of the pale blue dupion
45 x 25cm (18 x 10in). Cut a piece of the gold
dupion 130 x 25cm (51 x 10in). Pin, baste
and machine stitch these together along one
short side in order to make the base for the
embroidery. Repeat to make the lining for the
finished wrap. Allow a 1.5cm (⅝in) seam.

2 Throughout the project, you may find it
helpful to refer to *fig 1*. Begin with the gold
pleats by cutting a piece of gold organza
80 x 25cm (32 x 10in). Set the machine for
straight stitch and thread up with pale blue
thread in the top and bobbin. Set the stitch
length to 2.5. Fold the short edge of the fabric
under by 2cm (¾in) and sew a 1cm (⅜in)

seam along the fold. Fold down 2cm (¾in)
each time before stitching a 1cm (⅜in) seam
(*fig 2*). Continue until the 80cm (32in) length
measures 33cm (13in). Baste the pleats
before stitching if you prefer.

3 Iron gently on the reverse to straighten out
the fabric as it may begin to curl with the
pleats. Lay it onto the gold base fabric
1.5cm (⅝in) from the bottom edge and pin in
place. Stitch a wavy line to hold it in place at
both ends and stitch wavy lines in-between a
few of the pleats in order to hold the organza
to the base.

4 Pin and baste the coral organza onto the
gold base, slightly overlapping the raw edge of
the gold pleats.

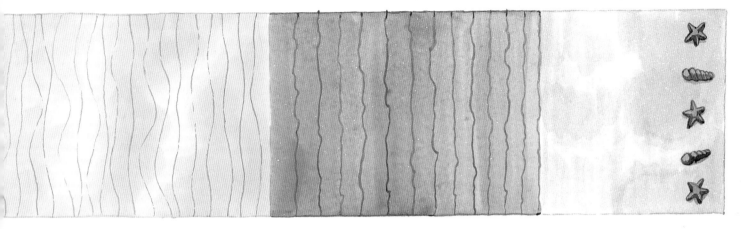

gold ripples   *blue waves*   *pale blue dupion*

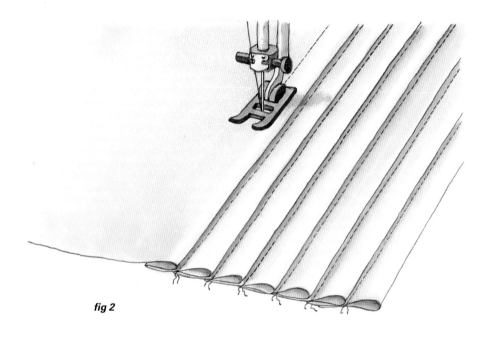

fig 2

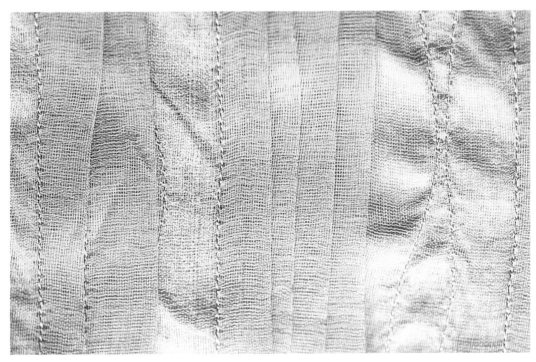

fig 3

6 Stitch a first line to hold the coral organza over the edge of the gold organza. Then begin to embroider wavy lines back and forth across the width. Keep the lines flowing and space them freely. Some lines can be close together before leaving a small gap and stitching lines further apart (*fig 3*). Continue until all the coral organza has been embroidered.

7 Cut the gold organza for the ripples 38 x 25cm (15 x 10in) and change the top thread colours to metallic turquoise and metallic blue. Repeat step 6 to embroider ripples on the gold.

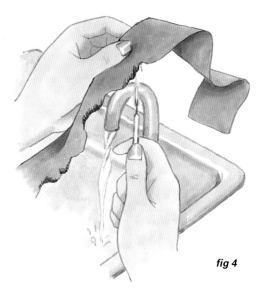

fig 4

5 Set the machine for twin needle stitching by changing the needle and using both turquoise and gold thread on the top. Use pale blue thread in the bobbin. Test the tension on a scrap of fabric first; adjust tension if necessary.

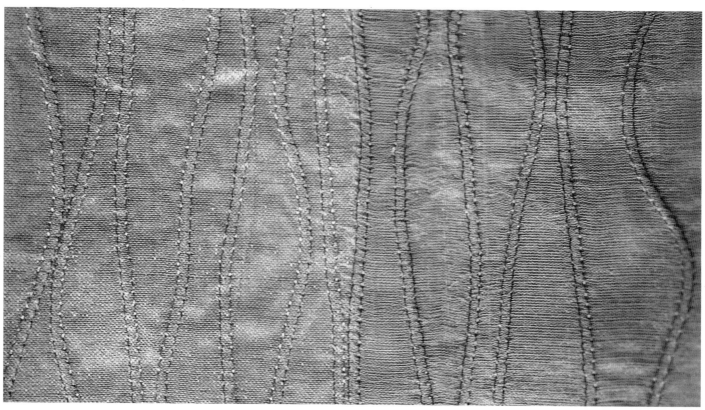

8 To make the blue wave section, cut the blue organdie into thirteen even widths of 5 x 25cm (2 x 10in). Then use a small cake candle to carefully burn one edge of each strip in order to make an uneven line. Brush ash off as you go and work above a sink in case of accidents (*fig 4*). Leave the tap running.

9 Lay the first wave onto the raw edge of the gold ripple and stitch using the same twin needle setting and threads as before. Lift up the wave, place the next wave 2cm (¾in) away from the previous stitching line and sew in place (*fig 5*). Continue doing this until all the waves are sewn down in an overlapping manner.

10 Note that the last section of the wrap remains as pale blue dupion (see *fig 1*).

11 Change the needle back to a single one and thread up the top and bobbin with an ordinary sewing thread in a matching colour to the gold dupion. Pin the embroidered length and the lining length right sides together, baste and stitch almost all the way around the wrap, leaving a small opening on one side. Seam allowances are 1.5cm (⅝in). Trim the corners and turn the wrap the correct way out through the opening. Slip stitch this opening, then carefully press all the seams.

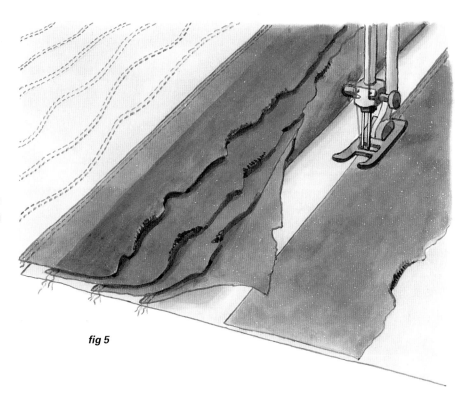

fig 5

12 If desired, hand stitch five decorative shell beads to each short edge of the wrap, positioning them at equal intervals. Or machine stitch simple shell motifs at these edges.

global
and ethnic

Above: *Stacked bamboo steam pots present a simplistic design repeat that could be interpreted in bands of appliqué or as a cross stitch border.*
Opposite page: top left – *Strings of beads enlivened with carved wooden animals create a visually stimulating picture ideal for use with hand embroidery;*
top right – *This hand-painted pot's stylized monkeys and grasses would work as a machine embroidered panel;*
below left – *Antique woven textiles offer ready-made design imagery combined with a delicately faded palette that translates well into fine hand embroidery;*
below right – *Hand-dyed fabric gives a project a more unique appeal.*

Folk culture offers a unique imagery that ranges from the simplistic to the truly opulent. For the embroiderer it inspires naive forms of intricate stitchery.

The twentieth century has seen many developments in communication technology, allowing us instant and easy access to countries and cultures previously thought distant and exotic. People travel further in search of exciting destinations or new experiences and all of that knowledge filters into the design process. Fashion designers look to other cultures for 'stories' or garment ideas and the richness of many exotic art forms enhances the work of contemporary embroiderers. Early travellers brought design ideas from the East to the West and techniques for embroidery and patchwork have travelled across continents and then back again in a revived form. They still do. Look out for beautiful woven silks from India, motifs from Chinese artefacts and even simple geometric designs from Scandinavia. And collect postcards and stamps from around the world. They will help you to build a unique colour palette, as well as provide a source of unusual images.

With a rich variety of travel and cultural books now available, and the opportunity to visit good museums, access to global information has never been easier. By developing your own collection of globally sourced images, projects can be enhanced and enriched and the finished appeal will be broader. Use this section to spark your imagination.

Right – *Coloured Moroccan tea-tumblers, hand-painted with accents of gold, present a decorative design starting point. Stitch using reverse appliqué techniques and richly coloured silks.*
Below – *This simple crafted metal and wood box lid shows an individual motif that could translate into various techniques either individually or as a repeat design.*

Opposite page: Top – *Endless design possibilities are created from Chinese joss papers. There are many colours and the method of printing onto them suggests translation in appliqué or layered appliqué;*
below left – *Handwoven fabrics are alive with design motifs and interesting colour combinations. They provide an ideal foil for opulent embroidery work;*
below right – *Hand-decorated papers are useful for collage projects. Layer them onto card and machine stitch.*

Left – Antique Indian textiles are beautifully crafted using tiny hand-embroidered stitches and fine silk threads. Practise copying fine stitchwork to develop your skill level.
Right – Fun ideas in bright colours can be drawn from unusual objects such as these little paper cocktail parasols. They offer a very pretty palette and a repeat design possibility when stacked together.

Opposite Page – This naive fish motif in battered metal would look good as machine embroidery combined with appliqué. It is ideal for small scale projects such as cards or tie backs.

Left – A papier mâché tiger can be stylized into either a fun motif for a child's project or developed into a more sophisticated image for use in furnishing fabrics. Combine with other animal motifs to expand the design possibilities.

Left – This close up detail of an ethnic textile demonstrates the use of a repeating motif. Some of the stitches have worn with age which only adds to the charm of any textile.
Right – Classic geometric motifs are to be found in this Persian carpet which would be suitable for interpretation into a canvas work project using richly coloured wools or silk threads.

Indian Evening Bag

This exotic evening bag combines many elements which were inspired by India, including the architecture, the fabrics and the spices. The fake shisha mirrors are created using foil seals from coffee jars – an innovative and effective touch. Once you start to experiment you'll find that many other everyday products can be used to great effect in embroidery projects.

Materials and Equipment
- 30 x 60cm (12 x 24in) piece of red chiffon
- 30 x 60cm (12 x 24in) piece of wine satin
- 20 x 114cm (8 x 45in) piece of wine chiffon
- 20 x 114cm (8 x 45in) piece of gold organdie
- 20 x 114cm (8 x 45in) piece of gold chiffon
- Anchor machine embroidery threads in the following colours: 1 reel each of orange 2285, yellow 2110, pink 2334 and red 2347
- 2.5m (2¾yd) length of yellow wool
- Sewing machine
- 18cm (7in) embroidery hoop
- Embroidery scissors
- Tracing paper
- Pencil
- Silver foil (coffee seals)
- Basic sewing kit (see page 136)

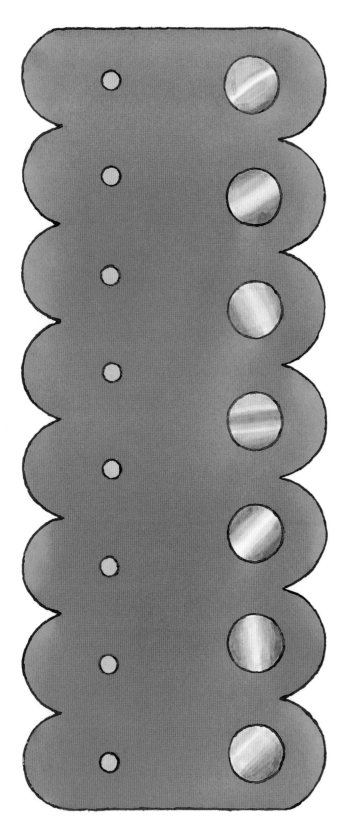

Template 1

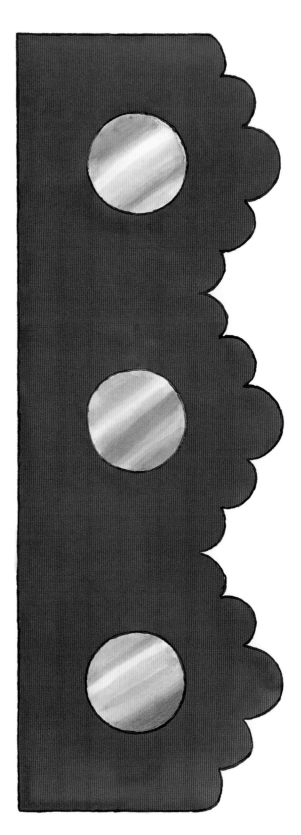

Template 2

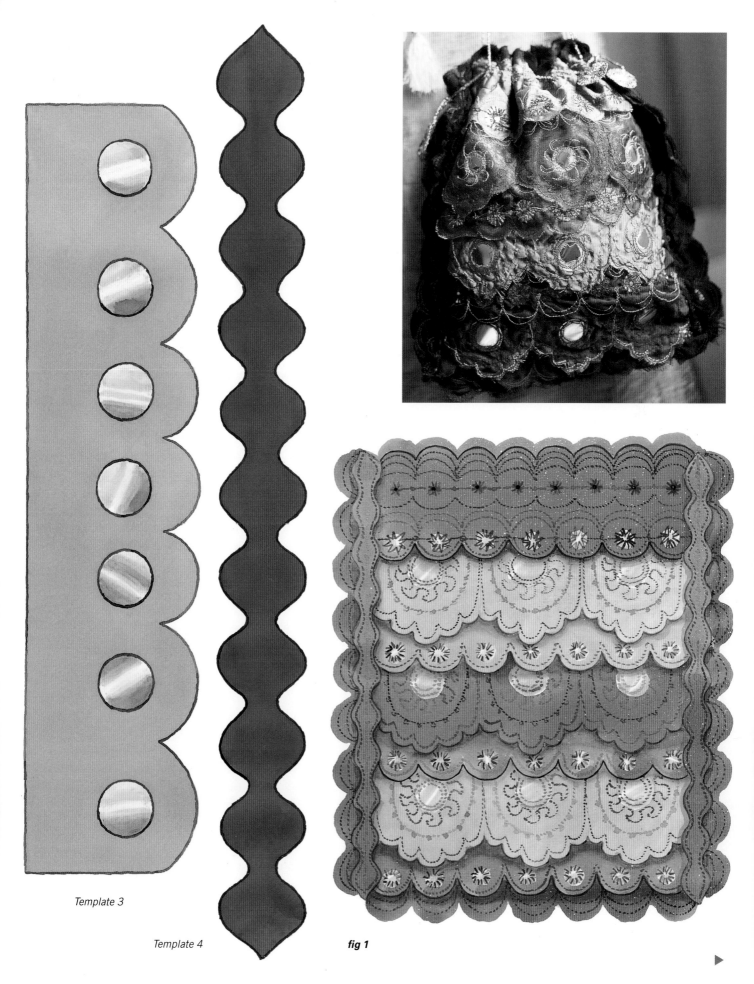

Template 3

Template 4

fig 1

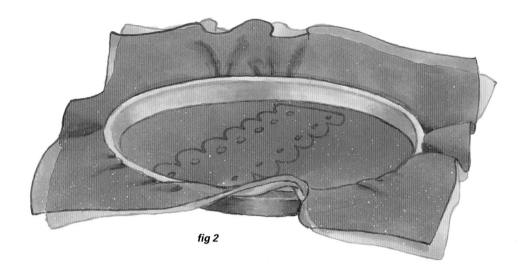

fig 2

Embroidery

1 Cut the red chiffon into two 30cm (12in) squares. Repeat for the wine satin lining, but place the lining to one side. Note that both sides of the bag are embroidered in the same way: you repeat steps 2–9 to make each side.

2 There are four main strips to embroider before they are trimmed and added to the red chiffon base. Template 1 (see page 80) is for a layer of gold organdie under wine chiffon. It has a position guide for seven foil circles and eight eyelet holes. Trace the template from the book, then trace directly onto the fabrics using a sharp pencil. (Most of the fabrics used are transparent.) Before you cut the fabrics, note that you will need to cut them larger than the templates traced in order to fit into the hoop (*fig 2*). Then cut seven foil circles, and pin and baste these onto the fabric, catching the edges of the foil only. Do not cut the eyelet holes at this stage.

3 Set the machine for free machine embroidery (see page 124), using orange bobbin thread and yellow top thread. Then place the two fabric layers cut from template 1 in the hoop. Follow the full colour diagram (*fig 1*/page 81) and begin by stitching the yellow scallop line and the sunburst detail around the foil 'mirrors'. Change to the red top thread and stitch the remaining scallop details. Ignore the eyelets – they will be stitched once the bag is lined.

4 Template 2 (see page 80) is worked in three different colour combinations (*fig 3*):
a: gold chiffon over gold organdie
b: a double layer of wine chiffon
c: a double layer of gold chiffon.
All colour combinations for template 2 have three 'mirror' suns on them. Trace and cut each fabric combination for template 2 as before, then cut, pin and baste three foil shapes onto each.

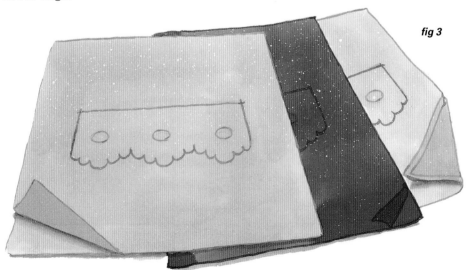

fig 3

5 Refer to the colour diagram (*fig 1*) in order to use the correct top colour of thread when you are embroidering each section. (The bobbin colour is always orange.) Stitch around each sun in a spiral direction before creating the rays. Change the top thread colour to stitch each bead line and change it again to stitch the scallop lines.

6 Template 3 (see page 81) has two colour combinations (*fig 4*):
a: gold chiffon over gold organdie
b: wine chiffon over gold organdie
Each requires seven foil circles. Trace and cut the fabric pieces as before, then cut, pin and baste seven foil shapes onto each.

7 Embroider the sunburst details onto the foil shapes on each section. Change the top colour to embroider the scallop details.

8 Use wine chiffon over wine satin to cut template 4 (see page 81). Cut two. These form the bag's side edging. Embroider the scallops only, using red for the top thread colour (refer to *fig 1*). The stitched bead detailing is added to these when the bag is made up.

9 Trim around the scallop stitch line of each template, cutting as close to the stitch line as possible. Lay them onto one of the red chiffon squares, placing as indicated on *fig 1*. Overlap the raw edges to conceal before stitching them down along the raw edge only, so creating a layered 'frill' (*fig 5*). When positioning, note that the three pieces for templates 2 and 3 are placed in alternate layers. Do not position the stitched pieces for template 4 at this stage.

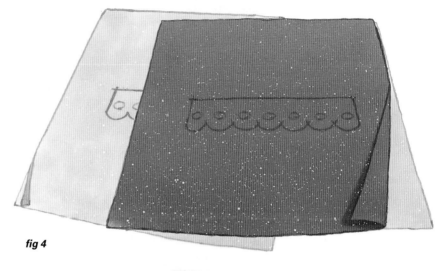

fig 4

fig 5

10 Now repeat the above, steps 2–9, to form the reverse of the bag. You may like to vary the colour combinations for the reverse.

▶

Bag Construction

1 Stitch decorative scallops around the base and sides of the two decorative panels before adding template 4 down each side to cover the edge of the embroidered strips. Machine stitch the bead detail onto template 4 through all layers of the panels.

2 To make up the bag, lay the two decorative panels onto the satin lining squares, wrong sides together, then pin all four squares together, embroidered sides out. Pin along the sides and the bottom before machine stitching close to the embroidered strips. Leave a small seam allowance all around. Cut around the edge of the bag, outside the stitched scallops.

3 The open top edge must be stitched as two separate pieces to finish. Use red top thread

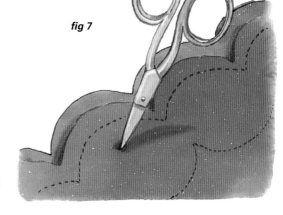

fig 7

and stitch three rows of scallops close to each other (*fig 6*). If you find it difficult to stitch this in a hoop, change to a normal presser foot.

4 To make the eyelets along the top edge (front and back) use the point of a small pair of scissors to pierce a hole through to the satin lining (*fig 7*). Make sure the hole is not too small as the decorative cord will have to be threaded through these to close the bag.

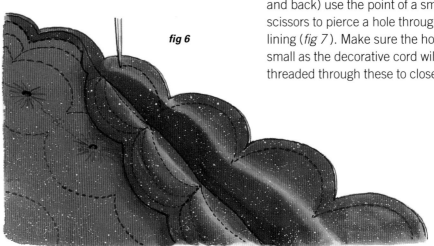

fig 6

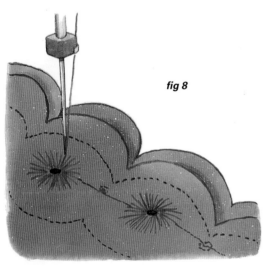

fig 8

5 Stitch back and forth in a sunburst pattern into the edge of each eyelet hole, stitching all around. Move the fabric along to the next eyelet hole by stitching a line, then a spiral detail, then a line (*fig 8*).

6 Make the decorative cord by re-setting the machine to normal and then, using the zigzag stitch, stitching over three strands of the yellow wool with red machine embroidery thread (*fig 9*). Cut the finished cord into two even lengths and thread (doubled) in and out of the eyelet holes.

7 Knot the cord ends and cover with a tassel or make foil suns. Tassels are made by wrapping a strip of card with machine embroidery thread before tying off one end and trimming the other (*fig 10*). Hand stitch each tassel to one end of the cord.

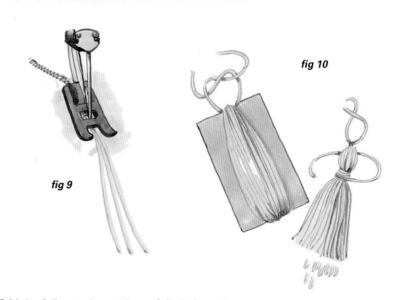

fig 10

fig 9

8 Make foil suns by cutting a foil circle and embroidering it as you did for the small sunburst foil shapes on templates 1 and 3. Hand stitch to the cord ends.

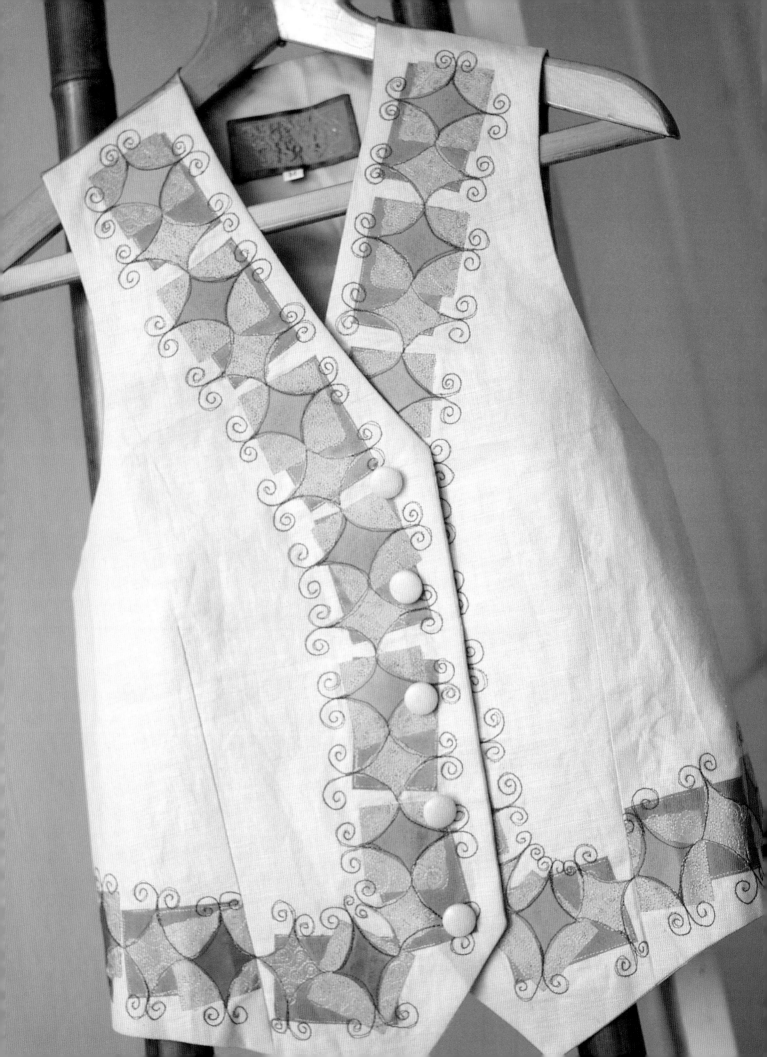

Chinese
Joss Paper Waistcoat

With their intricate inked patterns, fine neutral papers and panels
of leaf-metal, Chinese joss papers provide a rich source of design
inspiration. The contrasts in the colour and texture of these
papers are played out in this waistcoat using natural linen,
appliquéd opulent fabrics and delicate spiralling embroidery.

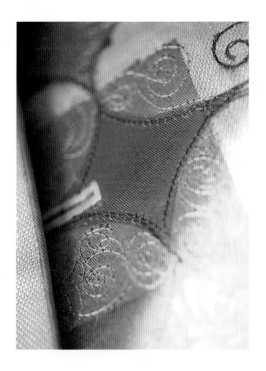

Materials and Equipment

- 1m (1⅓yds) natural beige
  linen, 114cm (45in) wide
- 2m (2¼yds) shot gold satin
  lining, 114cm (45in) wide
- 12cm (4¾in) orange chiffon,
  114cm (45in) wide
- 12cm (4¾in) shot green satin
  lining, 114cm (45in) wide
- 1m (1⅓yds) fusible interfacing,
  114cm (45in) wide
- 75cm (30in) iron-on fabric
  bonding 43cm (17in) wide
- Anchor machine embroidery
  threads: 1 reel each of cherry
  red 2347, yellow 2110 and
  bronze 2769
- Sewing thread to match lining
- Sewing thread to match linen
- Sewing machine
- 24cm (9in) embroidery hoop
- Embroidery scissors
- Waistcoat pattern enlarged to
  fit from templates on pages
  140/141
- 5 x 2.5cm (1in) cover buttons
- Iron
- Basic sewing kit (see page 136)

Template a

Template b

Template c

Embroidery

1 Trace off the waistcoat pattern given (see pages 140/141) and enlarge to the desired size following the instructions on page 138. Pin the front pieces onto the beige linen and baste around the pattern. Mark all edges and darts before removing the pattern.

2 Lay the fabric bonding over template **b** and trace eighteen shapes onto the paper backing. Space the motifs economically. Iron the fabric bonding onto the reverse of the shot green satin. Repeat for the shot gold satin, tracing fourteen shapes from template **a** and sixteen from template **b**, and for the orange chiffon, tracing eighteen shapes from template **c**.

3 Trim around the appliqué shapes, peel off the paper backing and lay the shapes, adhesive side down, onto the linen waistcoat fronts. Refer to *figs 1–3* to position before ironing in place.

4 Prepare the sewing machine for free machine embroidery (see page 124) and do some practice samples, creating spiral stitching on spare bits of fabric.

5 Thread up the machine with yellow top thread and bronze bobbin thread. Position a section of one linen front in the hoop, then place under the embroidery foot and lower the presser foot to activate the tension. Stitch around each orange chiffon shape (*fig 4*) but do not overstitch the motifs placed on top of these shapes. Then embroider all the gold areas, filling the centres with spirals.

6 Change the top thread to cherry red and embroider around the diamond shapes, creating spiral flourishes at the exposed ends. Complete the embroidery and press lightly with an iron on the reverse.

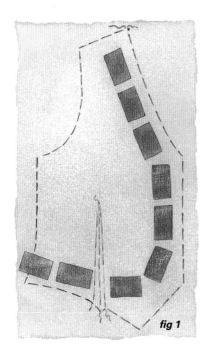

fig 1

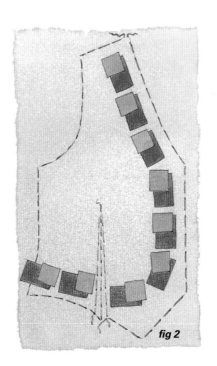

fig 2

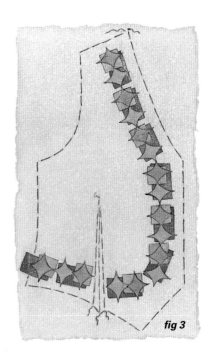

fig 3

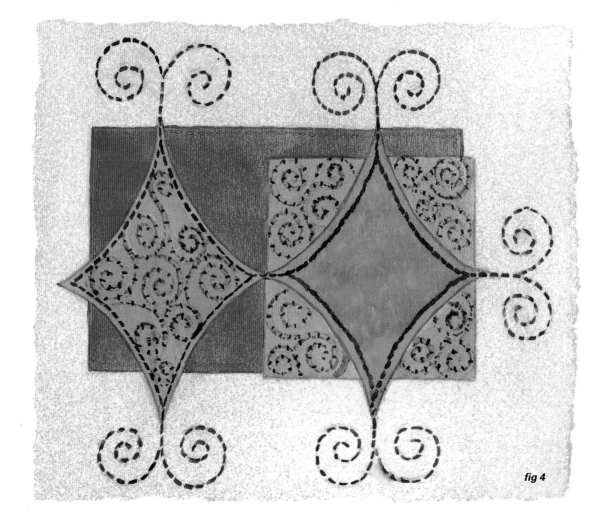

fig 4

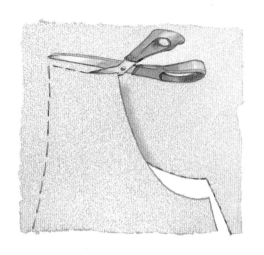

fig 1

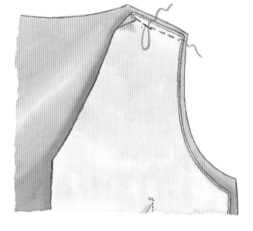

fig 2

Waistcoat Construction

1 Cut out the left and right waistcoat fronts following the basting lines (*fig 1*). Pin the pattern for the back against the fold of the shot gold satin fabric. Pin and cut two.

2 Cut two fronts and belt pieces from the gold fabric, marking the darts. Cut two interfacings for the fronts, again marking the darts.

3 Iron the interfacings to the reverse of the decorated fronts. Machine stitch the darts on the front panels and stitch the lining darts.

4 Baste, then stitch the shoulder seams together for the front and back panels (*fig 2*). Repeat for the lining. Note all seams are 1.5cm (⅝in). Press all seams and darts.

5 Fold the belt pieces in half lengthways with right sides together, pin, then stitch a seam around each, stitching along each angled short edge and along the long edge. Press, trim the corners, turn right side out and press again.

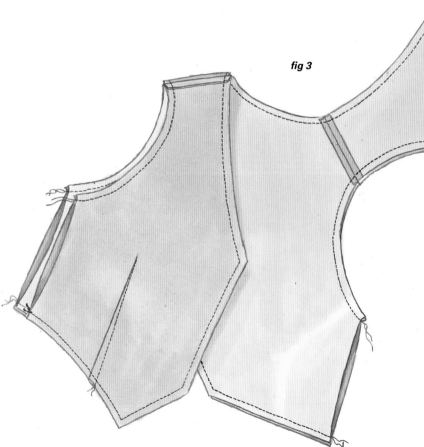

fig 3

6 Lay the fronts and gold satin lining pieces right sides together and pin around the edges, except for the side seams between the armhole and the lower edge. Stitch around all seams, leaving the sides open (*fig 3*).

7 Clip into the armhole curves and remove any bulk at the seams. Turn the waistcoat right side out by pulling the fronts through the shoulder channel and out through the open side of the back (*fig 4*). Press carefully.

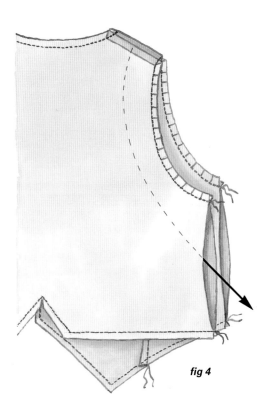

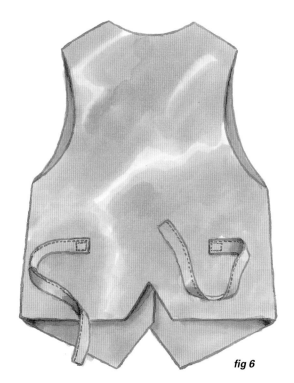

fig 4

fig 6

8 Place the side seams right sides together, pin from the armhole to the lower edge, baste and then stitch (*fig 5*). Press the lining side seam edges 1.5cm (⅝in) to the inside. Pin, baste and slip stitch together.

9 Fold the raw belt edges under 1.5cm (⅝in), press and pin on the back of the waistcoat at waist level, approximately 25 cm (10in) apart. Each belt piece should face the outside edge.

Top stitch a square on each to secure (*fig 6*) and knot the belt ends together.

10 Make five evenly spaced buttonholes on one front and attach five buttons covered in the linen onto the other front, making sure they correspond. Place buttonholes on the left side for male and the right side for female. Snip carefully into the buttonholes, from the centre to the edges, to open them up.

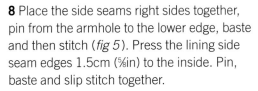

fig 5

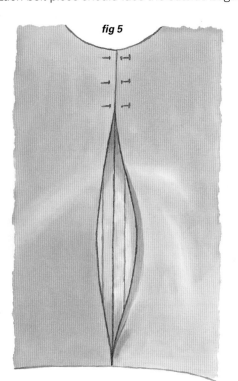

Naive Heart Cushion

American patchwork and quilting traditions have always appealed to me, and simple heart motifs are often used as a design source. Each heart on this cushion is slightly different but the design has harmony due to the neutral background colour.

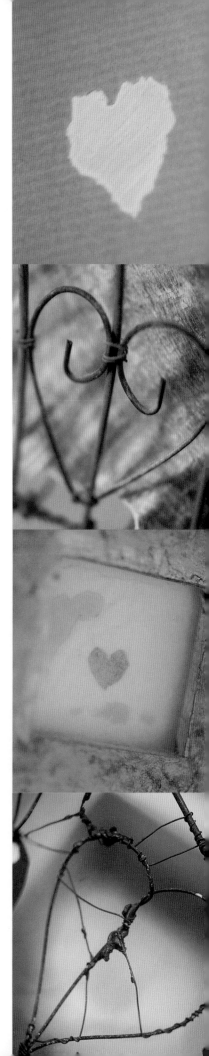

Materials and Equipment

- 45cm (18in) square of 14-count single thread canvas
- 43cm (17in) square of dark blue velvet
- Skeins as stated of tapestry wool in each colour listed in the key
- Tapestry needle, No. 20
- Tapestry frame
- 35cm (14in) square cushion pad
- Sewing thread to match
- Masking tape
- 48cm (19in) square of graph paper
- 45cm (18in) square of blotting paper
- 48cm (19in) square wooden board
- Drawing pins
- Basic sewing kit (see page 136)

2 skeins each of:

Colour	Anchor	DMC
Sky	8788	7802
Cyclamen	8414	7204
Fuschia	8458	7600
Candy	8422	7212
Violet	8528	7257
Teal	8630	7317

2 skeins each of:

Colour	Anchor	DMC
Peach	8308	7124
Lemon	8098	7784
Lime	9274	7584
Grass	8968	7545
Peacock	9004	7370
Moss	9214	7362

4 skeins each of:

Colour	Anchor	DMC
Cream	8040	7504
Coffee	8042	7473

GENERAL TIPS

• Enlarge the chart on
  a photocopier for
  easier working.
• Bind the edges of
  the canvas with
  masking tape.

Embroidery

1 Fold and mark the centre of the canvas vertically and horizontally with basting stitches. The black arrows on the chart indicate the centre of the canvas, and each square represents one half cross stitch.

2 Lace the canvas onto a suitable tapestry frame if you have one as this prevents too much distortion (*fig 1*).

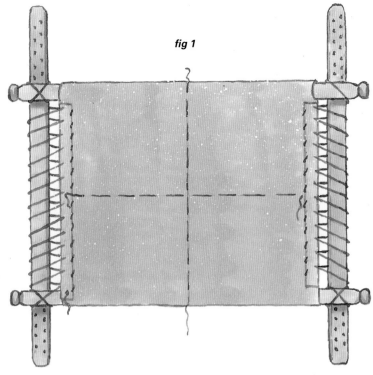

fig 1

3 Cut and thread an 45cm (18in) length of the central colour thread, then bring this through the canvas at the point that corresponds with the centre of the chart, leaving a 4cm (1½in) tail on the reverse. Re-insert the thread up to the right diagonally, across one canvas thread. Begin to half cross stitch, referring to the techniques section at the back of the book (see page 120) if necessary. To fasten off a thread, run it under the reverse of a few stitches. Darn under any 'tails' the same way.

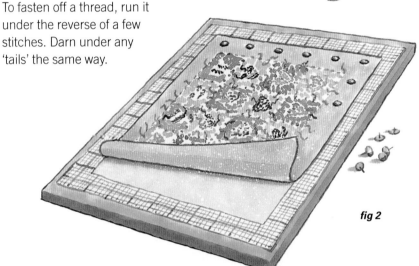

fig 2

4 On completion, the canvas may be distorted and may need to be blocked. Do this by laying a piece of clean blotting paper onto graph paper. The graph paper should be larger than the canvas. Lay the embroidery face-down on these, then use drawing pins to secure the three layers to a solid board. Use the lines of the graph paper as a guide to straighten up the edges of the canvas (*fig 2*).

5 Use a sponge and lukewarm water to *lightly* dampen the reverse of the embroidery. Leave to dry for a few days and repeat.

6 When dry, carefully remove the blocked embroidery from the board. Trim off excess canvas around the design, leaving 1.5cm (⅝in) of unstitched canvas all around. This is the seam allowance.

7 Place the canvas against the velvet backing fabric, right sides together. Pin, baste and machine stitch around three sides. Trim excess canvas and velvet from the corners, being careful not to cut into the stitching line, and turn the cover right sides out.

8 Insert a cushion pad before slip stitching the fourth side to finish.

food

Above: Simple stripes are created from tied bundles of asparagus with contrast shown in their textured heads. Interpret with hand embroidery.
Opposite page: top left – *Garlic heads are pretty to sketch once the papery skin is removed. Dry the skins and stitch as hand-made papers;*
top right – *Translate fresh parsley's rich colour and lacy-edged leaf into fine cutwork and hand embroidery;*
below left – *Chopped herbs could inspire a project using silk scraps and the trapped vermicelli technique;*
below right – *A flash of contrasting colour adds life to any imagery. Note how the pink raffia adds intensity to the green and white Chinese leaves.*

Abundant colour and natural forms contrast with the distinctive presentation and packaging that accompanies all varieties of food to form a wealth of design imagery.

Food has been used for many centuries as a source of design inspiration, probably because of the enormous variety of foods available and the vibrant colours and shapes. Fruit and herbs used whole or dissected create wonderful motifs that can be easily repeated to form an interesting design, and since nature created the colours the palette is usually in harmony. A picnic cloth embroidered with strawberries may be reminiscent of summers gone by, while herb motifs provide an appropriate and fresh decoration for table linen. Alternatively, glass jars of pasta or oranges stacked in a bowl offer interesting design possibilities in line and shape for decorating background areas, whilst rows of vegetables on market stalls are usually well presented and make an interesting visual reference. And recent developments in the standard of food packaging mean that labels, tins and wrappers should not be overlooked as a design source. Remember Andy Warhol's painting of Campbell's soup tins. Tie bundles of asparagus together with coloured string, sketch unusual foods like oysters or mussels, or open a packet of multi-coloured sweets and scatter them on a bright napkin. It's not hard to find contrasting colours, textures and shapes to play with.

Right – These ripe, richly coloured plums provide a satisfying colour palette. Slice open fruit to find an alternative source of design imagery.
Below – *Redcurrants are tiny but intense in colour. Crush and use to stain fabrics for a form of natural dyeing. Alternatively, interpret in stitch using French knots.*

Opposite page: top – *Shadow appliqué and machine embroidery are suggested by these delicately shaded clamshells overlaid with a pearlescent net bag;*
below left – *Three-dimensional appliqué would create a representation of an individual artichoke, or try stylizing the image using pintucks and grids;*
below right – *Piles of fruit create a stylized design in a strong palette. This would work as appliqué highlighted with hand embroidery.*

Left – Fiery red chillies are used fairly often as a design source. They interpret well into almost any technique but are particularly successful for hand embroidery.

Right – This bundle of herbs almost looks too good to use but the hand-tied effect with the herbs peeping out from the wrapping could almost be a form of three-dimensional appliqué.

Opposite page – Saffron has an almost thread-like quality and the most intense colour. It can be used to dye fabric a bright yellow. This shot clearly demonstrates the impact that is made by putting contrasting colours together.

Left – Lush ripe strawberries are a traditional favourite in all sorts of embroidery. Often used in Jacobean crewel work they lend themselves to hand embroidery and even cutwork.

Left – Succulent slices of pineapple are interesting when laid out and overlapped. The texture and colour contrast make for a simple yet stylish abstract design.

Right – Stems and buds in this wild asparagus make interesting proportions and could form a pretty border design for curtains.

Fruit Salad Sampler

On a hot summer's day a high spot must be a cool bowl of fresh fruit salad. These designs were based upon a cross-section of fruits such as star fruit and kiwi fruit as well as the more traditional oranges and lemons. The aim was to capture the colour and texture of these delicious fruits by using a rainbow of colours.

Materials and Equipment

- 35 x 45cm (14 x 18in) of white 14-count Aida fabric
- Skeins as stated of stranded embroidery cotton in each colour listed in the key
- Tapestry needle, No. 24
- Picture frame and mount to suit
- Backing board sized to suit frame
- Strong thread
- Drawing pins
- Masking tape
- Iron
- Basic sewing kit (see page 136)

Embroidery

1 Each square on the charts shown opposite represents either a block of Aida fabric or one cross stitch. The charts are shown individually and may be worked as such for use in greetings cards, but for the purposes of this project they should be spaced on one piece of fabric with a border around each one. Do this by dividing the Aida into six even squares by basting vertically down the centre, and basting one third up from the bottom and one third down from the top.

2 Use three strands of cotton for cross stitch areas and two strands for back stitch. The thread works best cut into 45cm (18in) lengths. Commence each design 5mm (⅛in) away from the corresponding basting lines, following the chart and key and referring if necessary to the stitch diagrams provided on pages 120/121.

3 When you start stitching, remember to leave a 4cm (1½in) thread on the reverse and catch this under the first few stitches (never tie a knot with this kind of embroidery). If you find it difficult to catch the thread while sewing, darn in the ends afterwards.

4 When you finish, remove the basting stitches, then press the Aida lightly on the wrong side with a cool iron and place onto a suitable backing board. Lace to the board by first securing at the top edge with drawing pins, then pulling the canvas firmly and pinning the lower edge. Now pin the side edges. The canvas should lie smoothly. Fold back excess canvas and lace the back from side to side, then top to bottom, using a strong thread (*fig 1*). Leave until you are ready to frame, then remove pins, mount and frame as desired.

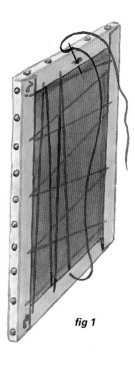

fig 1

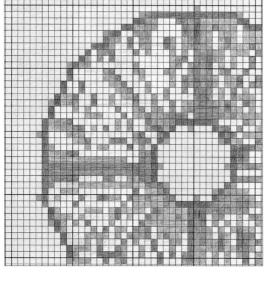

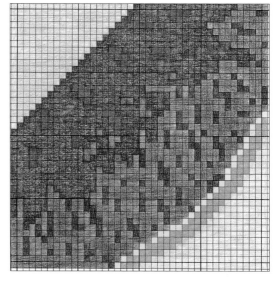

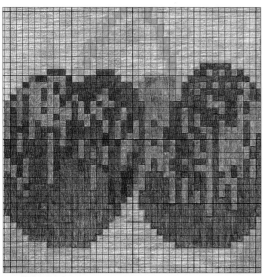

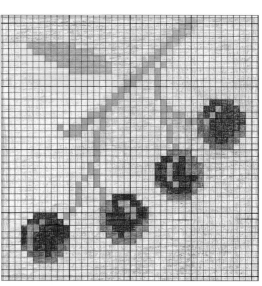

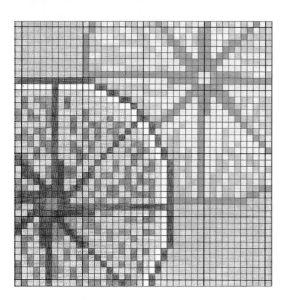

1 skein each of:

	Colour	Anchor	DMC
	White	1	White
	Violet	110	208
	Purple	112	333
	Pink	31	894
	Scarlet	47	321
	Bright yellow	303	742
	Tangerine	314	741
	Orange	324	721
	Cinnamon	326	720
	Grass green	225	703
	Emerald	227	701
	Aqua	186	959
	Apple green	204	993

2 skeins each of:

	Colour	Anchor	DMC
	Cyclamen	89	917
	Gorse yellow	302	743
	Blue	175	794
	Parrot green	254	3348

GENERAL TIPS
- Enlarge the chart on a photocopier for easier working.
- Bind the edges of the Aida with masking tape.

Fruit Motif Shelf Edging

Antique, hand-embroidered projects such as shelf edgings, handkerchiefs and christening robes are always interesting, both because of the techniques used and because they provoke a curiosity about the original embroiderer. Fruit motifs were commonly used for these traditional pieces and they often incorporated cutwork, which I have used for this project.

 The delicate nature of the techniques is hard to recreate today and it is almost impossible to imagine doing embroidery by candlelight as our ancestors may have done. Cutwork is usually done with white thread on white linen but I have added a fresh green thread to give this project a contemporary twist.

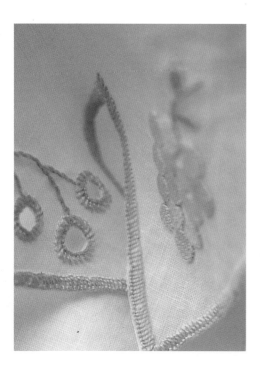

Materials and Equipment
- 80 x 33cm (32 x 13in) piece of white linen
- 10g ball of apple-green pearl cotton, No. 8
- Small embroidery hoop
- Hand embroidery needles
- Small embroidery scissors
- Tracing paper
- Pencil
- Masking tape
- Basic sewing kit (see page 136)

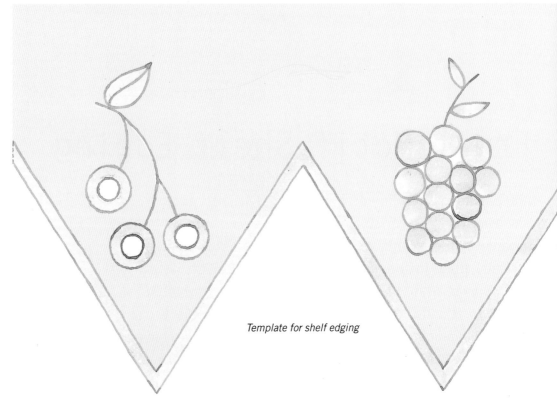

Template for shelf edging

Embroidery

1 The section of the edging shown in the template above can be repeated as often as required to fit the chosen shelf. (The project shown has three repeats.) Trace the template onto tracing paper. Then tape the linen right side up over the tracing, leaving a 2cm (¾in) gap from the bottom edge and a 4cm (1½in) gap from the side.

2 Trace the motifs onto the right side of the fabric, using a sharp pencil and marking all single and double lines. Trace the zigzag edging lines too. Repeat as desired (*fig 1*).

3 Tension the fabric in a hoop and embroider, using the above template as a guide. Refer if

necessary to the stitch instructions provided in the techniques section (see page 116). Start by satin stitching the leaves, working rows of adjacent straight stitches closely together across the shape. In a small area, such as a tiny leaf or petal, the stitches can go from edge to edge of the outline. You also need to satin stitch the insides of the grapes.

4 Now stem stitch the stems. Work from left to right (if you are right handed), taking small, regular back stitches that overlap slightly as you stitch along the line of the design. The thread should always emerge on the same side of the previous stitch so that all the overlaps lie in the same direction.

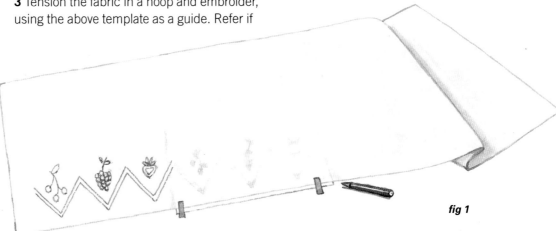

fig 1

5 The double lines are guidelines for buttonhole stitch. Do these areas next, including the zigzag edging. There should be a 4cm (1½in) gap between the end of this edging and the edge of the fabric.

6 Now cut away all areas surrounded by buttonhole stitch. These are the strawberry centres, the cherry centres and outside the zigzag edge (*fig 2*). Don't cut away the excess fabric at the top and sides of the motifs: this lies flat on the shelf.

7 Fill in the strawberry centres with a simple form of needlelace. Work on the reverse and run the needle under a few stitches before carrying it diagonally across to the other side of the strawberry. Run it under a few stitches again and bring it back to the first side a few stitches down (*fig 3*). Make sure you keep all these stitching lines parallel. The cross lines can be woven over and under the diagonal lines to secure (*fig 4*). Run all tails under a few stitches before trimming.

8 Double turn a seam allowance under the three edges that have not been buttonholed, slip stitch in place and press.

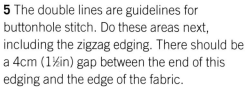

fig 2

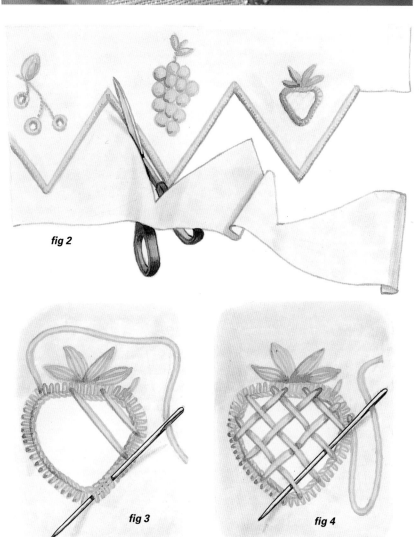

fig 3

fig 4

Herb Tablecloth

Herbs are wonderful in the way they combine colour, form and function. Think of the roasting red heat of the chilli pepper and the fresh green of an oregano leaf in contrast to its delicate pink flower. It was not difficult to conceive an object based on herbs that combined these elements. It resulted in this hand-embroidered tablecloth that is also reminiscent of traditional Chinese embroidery.

Materials and Embroidery

- 114cm (45in) square of green shaded chiffon
- 114cm (45in) square of white cotton lawn
- **or** 114cm (45in) square of hand-painted cotton lawn
- 5m (5½yd) length of green satin bias binding
- Skeins as stated of stranded embroidery cotton in each colour listed in the key
- Green handsewing thread
- 24cm (9in) embroidery hoop
- Embroidery scissors
- Embroidery needles (assorted)
- Tracing paper
- Pencil
- Anglepoise lamp
- Basic sewing kit (see page 136)

1 skein each of:		
Colour	**Anchor**	**DMC**
Red	46	3801
White	2	White
Pale pink	95	211
Cream	275	746
Pink	96	554
Light brown	349	301
Rose	969	223
Blue green	876	502
Pale rose	968	761
Grass	255	907
Purple	119	3746
Sage	261	368
Mid-green	214	3814
Light sage	264	3348
Spruce	216	3816

2 skeins each of:		
Colour	**Anchor**	**DMC**
Lime	254	3348
Pine	266	470

Oregano motif
Colours: light brown, lime, pale pink, pink,
pine and white

Stitches:
Leaves – *satin stitch*
Stems – *stem stitch*
Flowers – *detached chain (daisy stitch)*

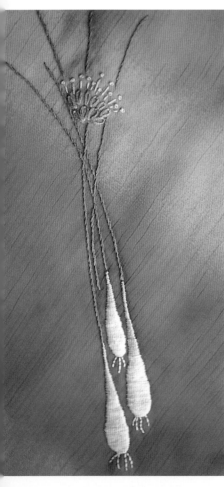

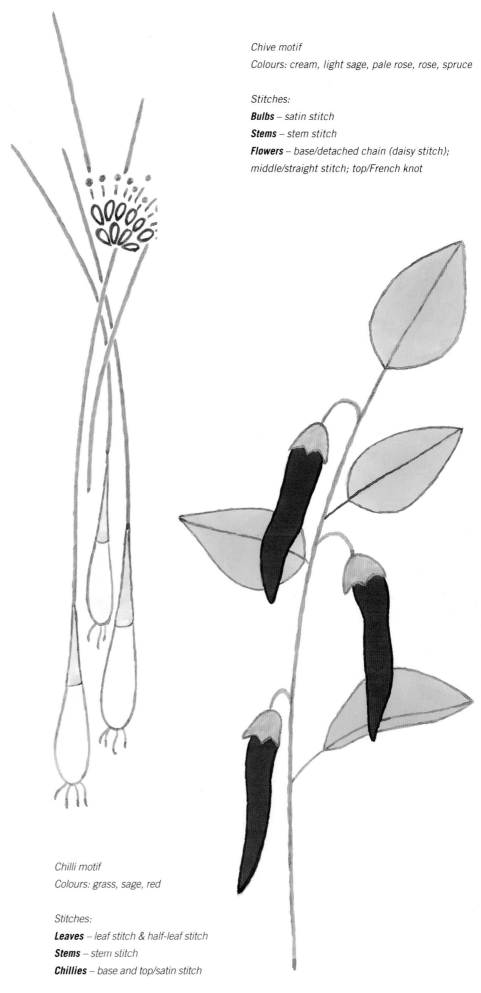

Chive motif
Colours: cream, light sage, pale rose, rose, spruce

Stitches:
Bulbs – satin stitch
Stems – stem stitch
Flowers – base/detached chain (daisy stitch);
middle/straight stitch; top/French knot

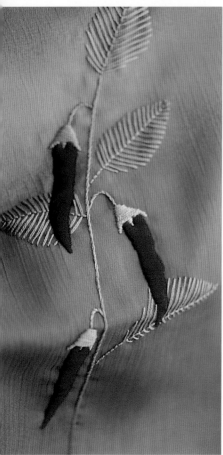

Chilli motif
Colours: grass, sage, red

Stitches:
Leaves – leaf stitch & half-leaf stitch
Stems – stem stitch
Chillies – base and top/satin stitch

Embroidery

1 Lay the chiffon over the cotton lawn and smooth as flat as possible. Baste through the centre, horizontally, vertically and diagonally in order to hold the two layers together. Baste around the outside edge.

2 Trace the motifs onto tracing paper, then reverse the paper and draw over the pencil lines. Use this reverse side to trace the motifs onto the reverse of the basted fabric with a sharp pencil. Follow the layout diagram provided (*fig 1*) and use a light box if possible or shine a lamp under a glass tabletop. Work the project with an anglepoise lamp upturned under the hoop to shine the template lines through.

3 Use two strands of thread for the embroidery, cutting each no longer than 45cm (18in) to prevent it from fraying and knotting. Interlace all thread ends under a few stitches on the reverse to secure, and work in an embroidery hoop to ensure an even fabric tension.

4 For each motif, refer to the relevant colour diagram and photograph for the stitches and colours required. Refer to the techniques section at the back of the book for advice on specific stitches. It is worth practising all stitches first in order to achieve the correct tension. Some stitches benefit from a slightly more random effect (e.g. detached chain stitch and buttonhole eyelets), but satin stitch should be smooth and neat and it may require patience to achieve the proper finish.

Juniper motif
Colours: blue green, mid-green,
light brown, purple

Stitches:
Leaves *– elongated detached chain stitch*
Stems *– stem stitch*
Berries *– buttonhole eyelets*

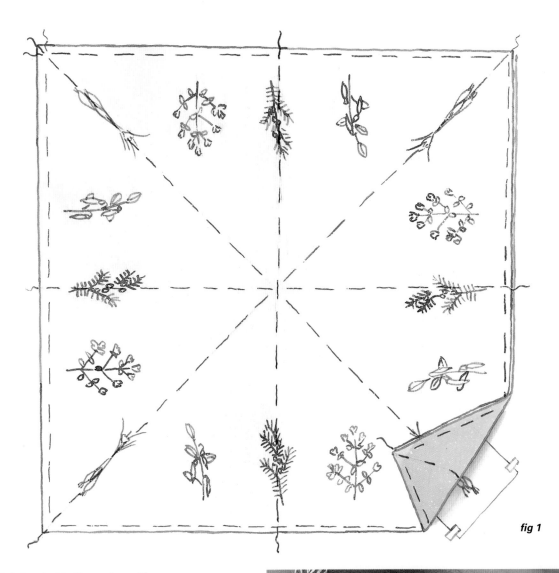

fig 1

Tablecloth Construction

1 On completion of the embroidery, pin bias binding around the raw edge of the tablecloth. Fold it under where the ends meet (*fig 2*), then slip stitch all around to finish.

2 Remove all basting stitches and press lightly on the reverse with an iron.

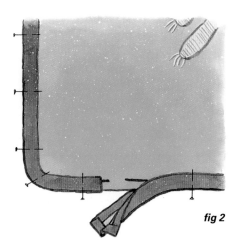

fig 2

techniques, materials and equipment

The sheer variety of fabrics and products on the market nowadays can be overwhelming. This chapter breaks down some of the most used and quoted techniques, materials and equipment in embroidery and, hopefully, simplifies them.

It should not be necessary to rush out and buy lots of specialized equipment to begin the projects in this book as much of the equipment required can be found in most domestic sewing boxes. As your interest grows, it is a good idea to look out for specialist fairs that demonstrate and sell fabric and equipment. You can usually pick up more unusual products and fabrics from these outlets, and often at discounted rates. Large items such as sewing machines should be thoroughly experimented with before you buy – most retailers are quite happy to let you try out free machine embroidery techniques in the shop first.

All the techniques used in the book are featured individually in this chapter, with simple stitch samples demonstrating clearly how each basic technique should look. Refer to this stage first and try it out before proceeding with a project, particularly if you are new to a style of embroidery. Practise does make perfect and it will help build confidence. You will not find every technique easy to master, as people are naturally more responsive to some working methods than others. Take things slowly, prepare well and have all materials to hand before you try.

Freestyle Hand Stitch

Hand stitches can be used to enhance any number of projects and can also be incorporated with appliqué and machine embroidery techniques. Most are a combination of either straight stitches or loops. Varying the colour and texture of the threads used adds more scope for design.

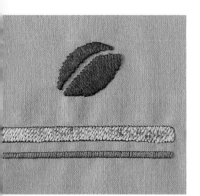

Satin Stitch
Make rows of adjacent straight stitches, working them close together across the shape required (a). The shape can be padded to give a raised effect by first putting some small, evenly spaced running stitches across the area at right angles to the satin stitch (b). Take care to keep the edges even.

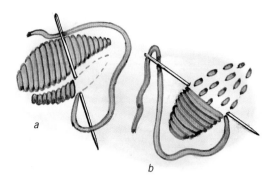

Chain Stitch
Bring the thread out onto the surface of the fabric and create a small loop with your thumb while inserting the needle where it last emerged. Then bring the needle out a short distance away, passing it over the loop (a). Hold the emerging thread to the left, form a new loop and repeat again. The stitches can be worked in curves (b) or straight rows (c) or used as a filling stitch.

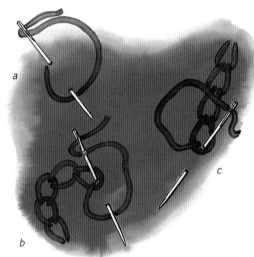

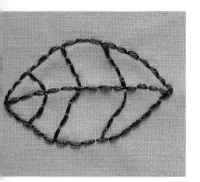

Back Stitch
Bring the thread through on the stitch line, then take a small backward stitch through the fabric. Bring the needle through again a little in front of the first stitch, and take another backward stitch to fill the gap. Keep the stitches small and even.

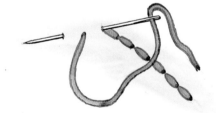

Stem Stitch
Work from left to right, taking small regular back stitches that overlap slightly as you stitch along the line of the design. The thread should always emerge on the same side of the previous stitch so that all the overlaps lie in the same direction.

Leaf Stitch

Bring the thread up through the fabric at point W and make a diagonal stitch to point X. Bring the thread through at Y and make a diagonal stitch to Z. Bring the thread up through the fabric just above W, pass it back down through the fabric just above X (a), and continue in the same way, working stitches on each side until the shape is lightly filled (b).

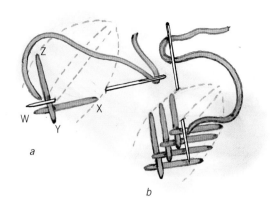

Couching

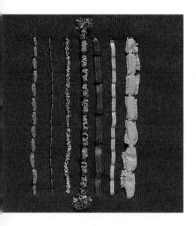

Couching is a way of introducing another thread into a design that may be too thick or impractical to stitch through the fabric. Lay the thread to be couched onto the surface of the fabric, following the line of a design. Thread the needle with the decorative thread and begin to overstitch the couched thread through to the fabric. Interesting effects can be achieved by using contrasting colours and textures. Use it to outline appliqué or to interpret designs such as landscape scenes.

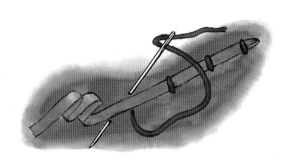

Daisy Stitch

Work as for chain stitch but work individual stitches around a centre point (a) to form petals. Finish each by taking a small stitch at the foot of the loop (b).

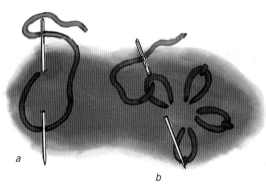

French Knot

Bring the thread out where the knot is required, hold it down with your thumb (a) and encircle the thread twice with the needle (b). Still keeping the looped thread taut, twist the needle back to its starting point and insert it close to where it first emerged (c). Pull the thread through to the back and overstitch to secure a single French knot or work several in succession. Use French knots to fill flower centres, as shown in the photograph of daisy stitch above, or to add a spark of colour to a design.

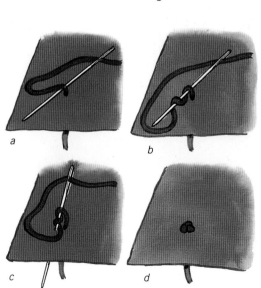

Canvas Work

There are many and varied canvas work stitches and often the same stitch will have a different name depending on the source of reference. Working methods may also vary and it's worth experimenting to find variations and combinations of stitches.

Half Cross Stitch

Half cross stitches are worked over one diagonal intersection of canvas thread. Bring the thread out on the lower left and re-insert diagonally one thread intersection up to the right. Now bring the thread through one canvas thread straight below and repeat (a). The reverse of the canvas should show rows of straight stitches. To change rows bring the thread out again, lower left but diagonally stitch one thread intersection down to the left (b). Work this row from right to left (c). Run thread ends through the reverse of the stitches to secure.

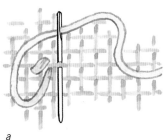

a

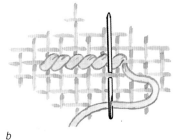

b

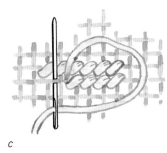

c

Cross Stitch

Bring the thread to the surface from the lower right-hand side and re-insert the needle two threads up and two threads to the left. Bring it out two threads down to form a half cross stitch (a). Bring the thread from the bottom left two threads up and two threads to the right and re-insert (b). This forms the top half of the cross stitch. With single-colour blocks it is faster to work a row of cross stitch, working each stitch over one Aida intersection, before returning and working the upper crosses (c). Always work stitches in the same direction.

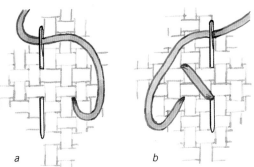

a

b

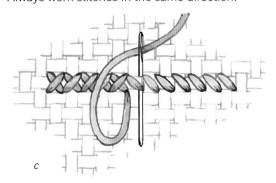

c

Trammed Tent Stitch

Tent stitches are worked over one diagonal intersection of canvas thread. Bring the thread out on the lower left and re-insert it diagonally one thread up to the right (a). Pull gently to tighten. Bring the thread through to the surface one thread intersection to the left of the first stitch and re-insert as before. Continue working the stitches as shown in *figs b–c.* The back of the stitched canvas should have longer diagonal stitches than the front. To make the design more hardwearing use a double thread canvas and stitch short lengths of thread down first before tent stitching over them (this is a similar technique to couching – see page 119).

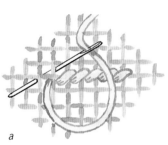

a

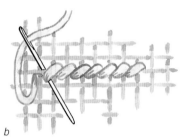

b

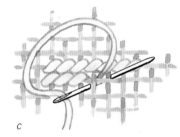

c

Back Stitch

Bring the thread out and re-insert one thread to the right (a). Bring the thread to the surface again one thread to the left of the completed stitch and re-insert into the original point (b). Bring the thread up again one thread to the left of the last stitch and continue in the same way to form a row of stitches (c). Follow the back stitch lines on a chart to change direction, working diagonally across the canvas if necessary and always using one canvas intersection for one stitch. To fasten off a thread, run it under the reverse of a few stitches.

a

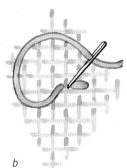

b

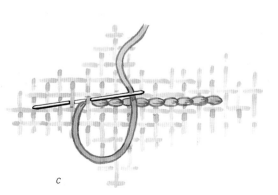

c

Hardanger

Hardanger is a traditional Norwegian technique based on blocks, known as Kloster blocks, cut areas and fine filling stitches. Although it is usually stitched white on white, the modern approach is to introduce colour either through the fabric, threads or both. It is fairly simple and quick to work and as hardwearing as cross stitch for projects such as cushions.

Satin Stitch (Kloster) Blocks

Hardanger is worked with rows of straight stitches in groups on the canvas. The stitched blocks always consist of an odd number of stitches over an even number of fabric threads and the stitches may be worked from left to right or right to left. For the Hardanger project in this book (see pages 46/49), work seven stitches over six fabric threads to form each block, leaving a centre square unstitched. Catch all thread ends on the reverse of the blocks to secure. The unstitched centre can be carefully cut away to create an open-work effect and then decorated with a fine stitch such as dove's eye filling.

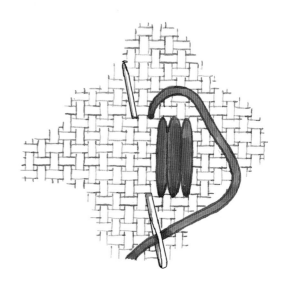

Dove's Eye Filling

This lacy filling loops over the cut satin stitch blocks. It is composed of four looped stitches, one on each side of the space left by the cut fabric threads. Bring the thread through from the reverse of the top row next to the central satin stitch and close to the cut edge. Gently loop the needle under the middle stitch of the next row (ninety degrees around the cut block) and form the top of a figure of eight before moving to the next satin stitch row. Continue to loop the thread under the centre stitch of all four rows. On reaching the last row, insert the needle on the opposite side of the satin stitch to where you started and take the thread right through to the reverse to finish. Secure tail ends under stitches on the reverse.

Remember, the figure of eight loops are stitched only onto a single satin stitch, not all the way through to the reverse – except when starting and finishing the block.

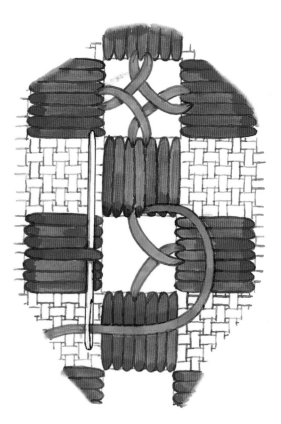

Cutwork

Cutwork is traditionally worked on white fabric with white thread. Areas of the design are stitched before the fabric can be cut away to create an open effect. The traditional cutwork outline stitch is buttonhole stitch which you may wish to pad out by first sewing a running stitch between the double lines of the design.

Buttonhole Stitch

Bring the thread out on the inner line. Insert the needle in position on the outer line then take a straight downward stitch. The point of the needle must emerge over the loop of thread (a). Pull through to secure and repeat, keeping the stitches close together (b). The looped edge is the one that you cut to.

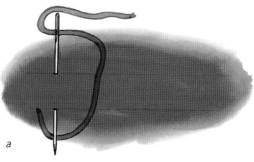

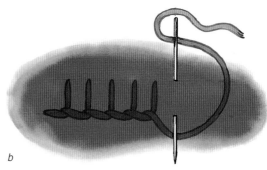

a

b

Buttonhole Bars

The bars are formed by first taking a large straight stitch across the width of the design and then taking the stitch back to the original point (a) – i.e. to form two straight stitches.

Buttonhole stitch over the loose threads, taking care not to pick up any of the background fabric (b). Only trim fabric away once the outline buttonhole stitching has been done (c–d).

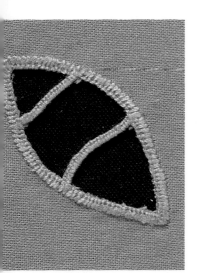

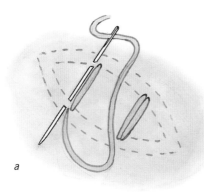

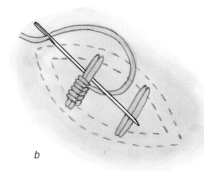

a

b

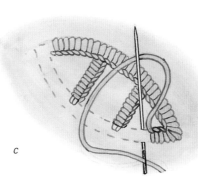

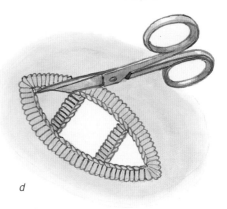

c

d

Free Machine Embroidery

Free machine embroidery allows you to stitch in any direction, smoothly building up textures and basically drawing with the machine. Techniques such as appliqué can be enhanced with machine embroidery and there is a huge variety of machine threads on the market, each with a specific use. It is a case of trial and error to find the threads that work best with your machine.

Setting Up

You will need an embroidery hoop in order to tension the fabric when free machine embroidering: I prefer to use wooden hoops, as although slightly bulky they keep the fabric taut. The new spring-loaded plastic/metal hoops allow for easy repositioning of fabric but the tension is not as good.

The fabric must be tautly held in the embroidery hoop for successful free machine embroidery. It is often worth taking an additional step and binding the hoop's inner ring with a strip of cotton fabric to prevent the fabric from slipping.

Do be aware that not every machine will easily do free embroidery. Note that there are different types of presser foot, and modern machines usually have a number of different types. Your machine may not have a darning/embroidery foot attachment, but it is possible to stitch without a foot and use a bare needle – it just needs practise and great care. If you do not have a darning foot, do not bring your fingers anywhere near the unprotected needle when stitching. Keep them outside the embroidery hoop.

Preparing the Machine

There are some basic steps to take in order to set up your machine for the techniques which follow. Once you have set it as instructed below, try the two techniques described on the opposite page.

1 Lower the feed dog (zigzag teeth) if possible or cover with a darning plate if you have one. If not, clear sticky tape stuck down over the feed will also do.
2 Set the stitch width dial to zero.
3 Set the stitch length dial to zero.
4 Check the tension in the bobbin and top thread according to the manufacturer's recommendation. The top tension should be set in the middle of the dial and the bobbin thread should come away when tugged.

It should not run freely unless you are trying whipping stitch.
5 If your machine has programmed stitches, set it for straight stitch.

Using Free Machining for Colouring

It is possible to add texture and solid areas of colour with free machine embroidery – and it is a much quicker method than using appliqué techniques.

Practise building up solid shapes or areas of colour simply by stitching back and forth over your fabric, using the needle as if it is a coloured pencil. A common mistake is to overstitch on the one spot and if this happens the fabric may distort badly or the thread may break, both of which can be very frustrating to the novice machine embroiderer, but you will soon learn to avoid this.

Other Techniques with Free Machining

Once you have built up a little skill, it is also possible to free machine using a zigzag stitch to build up small solid blocks and wavy lines of colour. And by turning the stitch width dial as you sew, lines of varying width can be created. Always sew slowly and carefully when using this technique.

TIPS

If you find problems occurring once you start stitching, check the following points:
- the presser foot has been LOWERED
- the needle is sharp – change for a new one if necessary
- tension in the top and bobbin
- the fabric is tight enough in the hoop
- some metallic threads work better if the top tension has been slackened off a bit

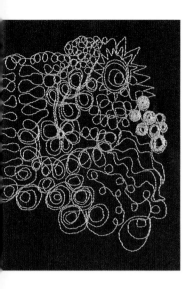

Doodling

Frame the fabric in an embroidery hoop and lay the flat of the fabric against the bed of the machine. Turn the needle control to pick up the bobbin thread, bringing it through to the surface. Then re-insert the needle into the fabric and lower the presser foot lever even if you are using no presser foot. Now begin to stitch by slowly pressing the foot pedal and moving the hoop, keeping your hands either side of the hoop. Press the pedal harder but keep the hoop moving – move it slowly to keep the stitches small. By moving the hoop faster, large jagged stitch effects can be created. Stitch back and forth in order to build up areas of colour or stitch freely in any direction, overlapping the threads. Trim excess threads off close to the fabric surface. The smaller the stitch, the less likely the cut thread will unravel.

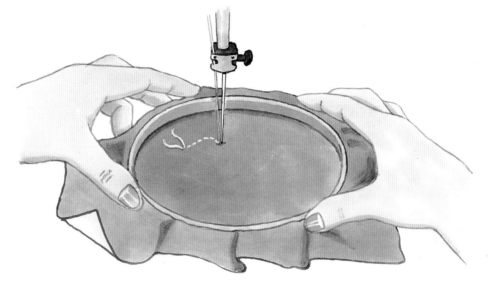

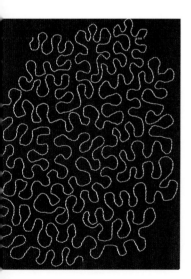

Vermicelli

Vermicelli is Italian for 'small worms' and this stitch allows for a pattern to be built up by stitching in and out of small wavy lines. Place the fabric in an embroidery hoop to ensure correct tension and thread up the machine for free machine embroidery. Stitch back and forth continuously in waves, taking care not to overlap any lines. Ensure all the background fabric is covered with stitched lines. To make the surface more interesting use a variegated colour thread. (See also Vermicelli with Trapped Fabrics on page 129.)

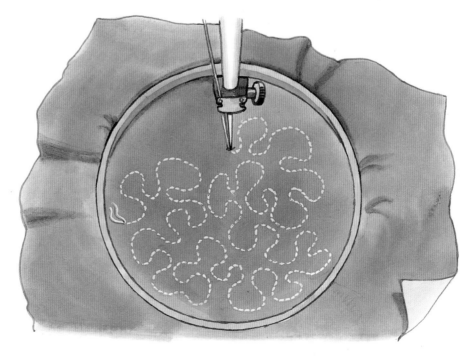

Hand Appliqué

Appliqué was originally the name given to patches of fabric stitched over tears or worn areas in a garment. Over the centuries it has evolved into a high level craft taking many forms. Hand appliqué can be versatile and practical. You may wish to use a hoop for ease.

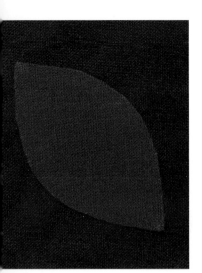

Turned Edge Appliqué

This technique works best with light- to medium-weight fabrics that do not fray. After choosing your appliqué shape, cut the fabric approximately 1cm (⅜in) larger all round than the finished size. Turn this seam under and baste in place (a). Pin the shape to the background fabric and slip stitch or stab stitch all around (b). Embellish with hand stitching (e.g. blanket stitch) if required.

In an alternative method, called needleturned appliqué, the shape is pinned on without the raw edges being basted under. The point of the needle is used to push the edge under as you stitch.

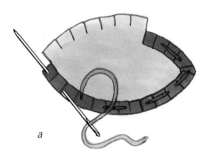

a

b

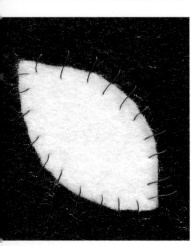

Inlay

Inlay involves the placing of one colour of fabric directly into the same space cut in the background of another colour. You will find that it works best on felt since felt doesn't fray and is thicker than most fabrics, allowing for ease of stitching.

First layer up two contrasting coloured squares of felt and use a sharp scalpel to cut a simple motif from both layers (a). Keep the motif whole – do not cut it in sections (b).

Now swap the motifs into the alternate hole (c) and slip stitch all around, stitching through the felt to hide the stitches (d). The stitches won't show as the felt is so thick. Squares of inlay felt can be stitched together to form a larger project.

a

b

c

d

Machine Appliqué

Machine appliqué is a development of machine embroidery and the speed at which you can achieve stunning results is very satisfying. Keep the stitches neat and close together so you can trim the thread ends back to the surface without fear of them unravelling.

Fabric Bond Appliqué

Layers of colour can be built up and overlapped using this technique. It also prevents fabric from fraying and slipping and so is ideal for fabrics which are otherwise difficult to apply. Begin by ironing a layer of fabric bond onto the reverse of the fabric to be applied (a). Cut out the desired shape, peel off the paper backing from the bond (b) and place the motif glue-side down onto the background fabric. Iron in place (c). Now decorate with machine embroidery (d). Try a few types of fabric bond to find out which kind suits your project best as sometimes the bond is very stiff and prevents the finished fabric from draping.

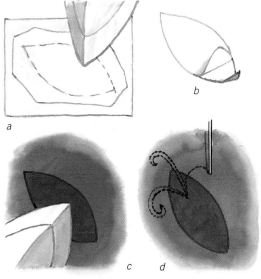

Reverse Appliqué

Layer up two or three contrasting fabrics in your embroidery hoop. It is best to choose light-weight fabrics since the finished piece will be quite heavy. Then embroider the areas to be cut twice (a); this double line of stitching helps to prevent the fabric from fraying.

Once the motif is complete, use small, pointed embroidery scissors to pick up each layer of fabric within the shape and trim it away. Experiment by trimming away alternate layers to make a design more interesting and to add depth (b). By layering up sheer fabrics, such as chiffons, many different colours can be used in the same design.

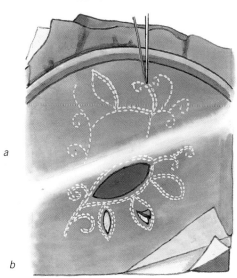

Satin Stitch Appliqué

Trim, pin and baste the chosen motif to the background fabric (a). Set the machine to normal and use the zigzag foot. Raise the feed dog if lowered, and set the stitch width to its widest setting and the stitch length to 0.5. Slowly satin stitch around the edge of the motif (b). Turn corners by keeping the needle in the fabric, raising the presser foot, turning the fabric, lowering the presser foot and then continuing to stitch. You may need to vary the stitch width and length in order to achieve a smooth satin stitch. It may also help to lower the top tension down by one in order for the thread to run through freely.

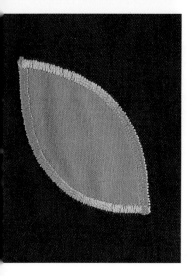

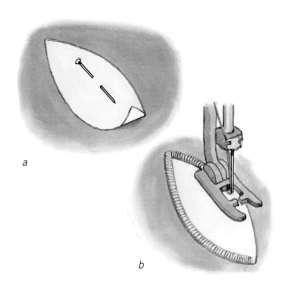

Three-dimensional Techniques

Some projects need a little extra texture in order to make them more interesting. One way to make a very basic fabric more exciting is to use pintucks. Appliqué shapes can then be added for more impact. Frayed edges are also useful in creating effect, either as a texture, a feature (e.g. grasses in a landscape), or simply as a way of developing a mistake! Always remember that sometimes the stitching that other people would call a mistake is just the texture or technique that an uninspired embroiderer is looking for!

Pintucks

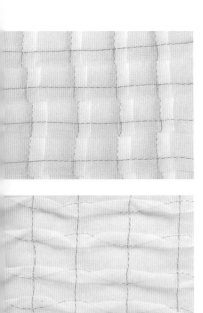

Pintucks are seamed ridges in fabric formed by folding the fabric over and machine sewing a seam line 1cm (⅜in) away from the fold, using the normal straight stitch foot. Continue to make folds and stitch in a lengthways direction. You can experiment by varying the width of the tucks and making the seam allowances larger or smaller. When stitched in rows, pintucks can be caught down afterwards with rows of straight stitches going in alternate directions (a). Or try turning the pintucked fabric ninety degrees, then pintucking again to form a decorative, raised grid (b).

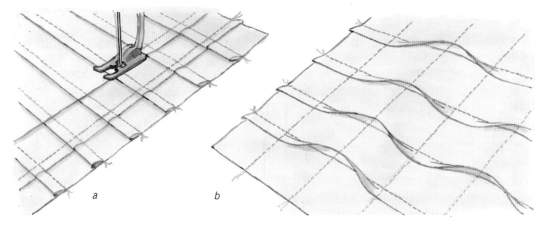

a   *b*

Twin Needle Stitching

You can buy twin needles in a variety of stitch spacing and the effect they produce looks like a finer version of pintucking. Thread each needle individually and begin to sew lines using a straight stitch (a). By guiding the fabric you can sew wavy lines instead of straight ones. For greater impact, try using contrasting coloured threads (b).

Note: Do not try to free machine embroider with a twin needle. You may break the needles.

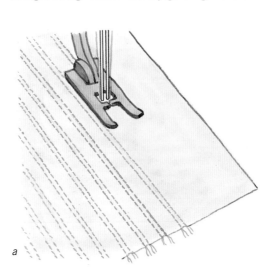

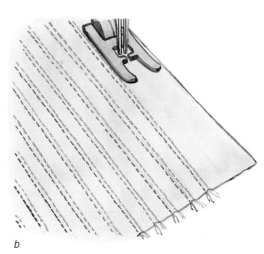

a   *b*

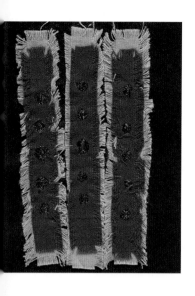

Fringed Layers

Place three layers of fabric in an embroidery hoop, preferably choosing something that will fray quite easily. Machine stitch lines or stitch a motif in rows, leaving gaps for the 'fringes'. If the fabric has an open weave or is particularly fine, double stitch all lines in order to prevent it from fraying back too much. Then, using sharp, pointed embroidery scissors, cut away one edge of the top fabric, cutting between the lines of stitching. Snip into it at regular intervals and fringe off. Try cutting away a whole length of the top fabric along the next line to reveal the next layer to be fringed and repeat the fringing process.

Three-dimensional Appliqué

This works well for natural motifs (such as flowers, insects, and fish scales, etc). Plan your motif as you would for ordinary machine appliqué but pinch it in a little by gathering or pleating by hand before stitching it down at one point only (e.g. the top of the fuschia cone as illustrated in figs a–c). You can press folds with an iron or baste to secure if preferred. Add extra detail with free machine embroidery before or after applying the appliqué.

a

b

c

Vermicelli with Trapped Fabrics

Scatter tiny fabric scraps onto a background fabric and use a close vermicelli stitch (see page 125) to hold them down. You may find it easier to secure the scraps in place with a little fabric glue before stitching.

Water Soluble Fabrics

With water soluble fabrics you can create a lacy look on a project without using bobbin lace. There is a variety of brands of water soluble fabric available and it's worth experimenting to find which suits your fabric best. Some dissolve better than others and give a different finish. Hot water soluble fabric tends to leave the thread softer, which is more suitable for fashion projects and delicate designs. Cold water soluble fabric is stiffer and is ideal for three-dimensional projects.

Hot Water Soluble Fabric

Work in an embroidery hoop to help tension the water soluble fabric. Set the machine for free machine embroidery (see page 124) and use an interesting, coloured thread in the bobbin and the top since both sides of the finished project will be seen. You can if you wish draw a motif onto the water soluble fabric first with a pencil or pen – either will dissolve.

Begin by outline stitching twice around the motif (a) and then infilling using wavy lines and scrolls and overlapping all the stitches. This is important as the final piece needs the stitches to link in order to hold together once the fabric is dissolved. But don't overstitch the motifs – you are aiming for a delicate effect.

To dissolve the fabric and leave the motif you will need a basin and a kettle of boiling water. Simply trim away any excess fabric, place the stitched motif in the basin and pour over boiling water until the fabric has dissolved and only the stitching is left (b). Pin the motif onto an ironing board to re-shape and iron dry. Alternatively, first pin the trimmed motif onto a polystyrene tray and then place the tray into the basin before pouring over the water. This helps the motif to retain its shape and minimizes shrinkage. Iron or leave to air dry.

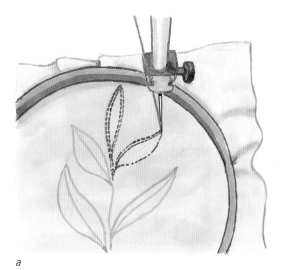

a

b

Cold Water Soluble Fabric

Work a motif on the fabric as directed for hot water soluble fabric. It is advisable to use a double layer of cold water soluble fabric as it does tend to tear with heavy stitching. Dissolve in a basin as before but this time using cold tap water. Iron or air dry.

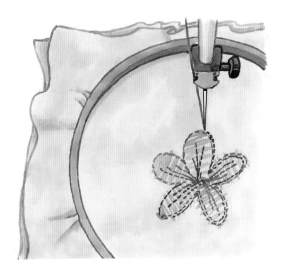

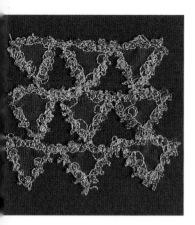

Water Soluble with Trapped Fabrics

This technique allows solid areas of colour to be incorporated into a design. Plan the motif carefully and draw the motif onto hot or cold water soluble fabric. Place the fabric into an embroidery hoop, then pin scraps of fabric (any kind) onto the soluble fabric. Now stitch around each fabric scrap, catching the edges. Continue by adding decorative areas of stitching to the fabric edges. Finally, dissolve using the appropriate hot or cold water method and dry as before.

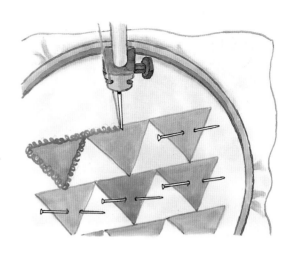

Water Soluble Beaded Edgings

With water soluble fabrics, it is easy to add a delicate lace border to collars, cuffs, scarves and around cushions. Start by choosing a simple motif to repeat and overlap. It can be an obvious shape such as a leaf or a random abstract.

Place your hot or cold water soluble fabric in the hoop and begin to embroider each motif individually until you have enough to fit the edge of your project. Leave a 'stem' on each motif of around 1cm (⅜in). Do this by stitching a line up and down from the top of your motif (a).

Once you have stitched and dissolved all the motifs with the appropriate method, small beads can be stitched on the edgings to enhance them. Use a beading needle and the same machine embroidery thread as the motif and stitch neatly over a small area of the motif, knotting the loose thread ends on the reverse.

Now lay the individual motifs along the edge of your unlined project – they must point inwards, with right sides down (b). Pin and baste in place. Next lay the lining and project right sides together, baste and sew around all the seams, leaving a gap in order to turn the project the right way out. Slip stitch the gap. The water soluble fabric edge should now hang freely, forming a unique trim (c).

a

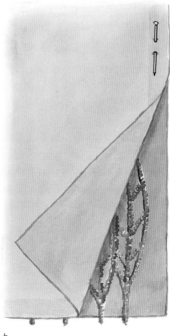

b

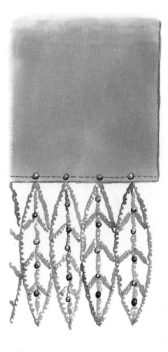

c

Textural Stitches

These machine stitches add a slightly raised quality to a design but they require practice to get them right. It is useful to have a spare bobbin case as you have to slacken off the tension screw and it can be difficult to adjust it back to normal stitch tension.

Cable Stitch

This technique allows for chunkier threads to be used that would normally be too thick to pass through a needle. The top thread should be a standard thread and the thick thread should be wound onto the bobbin. Slacken the bobbin tension screw to allow the thread to unwind freely. Stitch a motif as normal but remember that the correct side of the design is being worked upside-down so you are stitching the wrong side of the fabric. The stitch can be worked as free machine embroidery or with a presser foot.

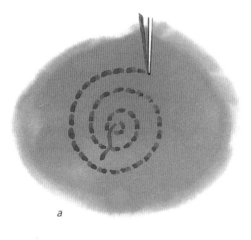

a

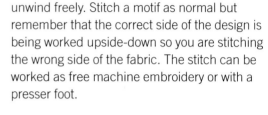

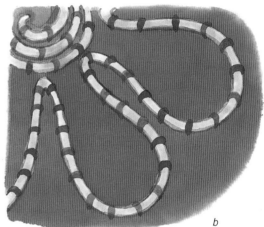

b

Whipping Stitch

Whipping stitch is a delicate version of cable stitch and is sewn as free machine embroidery. It works best in shiny rayon threads with contrasting colours in the top and bobbin. The stitch side that is seen is the side that is used. Slacken off the bobbin thread and slightly tighten the top thread. As you stitch, the bobbin thread comes through to the surface and wraps itself around the top thread. Depending on the speed at which you stitch, part of the top thread may or may not show.

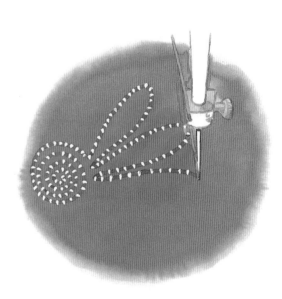

Dyeing and Colouring Fabrics

Commercial fabric colours are sometimes a little too flat and a project can look truly original if it is based on a hand-dyed fabric. There are many methods for dyeing fabrics and it takes time to find the method that you like or that will work for a particular project. I like to use Procion dyes but the quantity of dye powder required will vary from manufacturer to manufacturer. The following cold water method works best on natural fabrics.

Materials and Equipment

- 50cm (20in) square of cotton fabric
- Procion dye powder (assorted colours)
- Jam jars
- Plastic tubs and bucket
- Measuring jug
- Household salt
- Washing soda crystals
- Rubber gloves
- Metal tablespoon
- Metal teaspoon

Method

1 Soak your chosen fabric in hot water in order to remove any starch and to allow the dye take up to be consistent.

2 Mix up the salt and soda solutions in the quantities given below. **Remember** that the soda solution will be further diluted before use.
   Salt solution: 55g (2oz) salt to 560ml (20fl oz) hot water
   Soda solution: 110g (4oz) soda to 420ml (15fl oz) hot water

3 Use a jam jar and wear rubber gloves to mix the dye powder with hot water – try a teaspoon of dye powder to half a jar of hot water and add a tablespoon of salt solution. Stir well.

4 Place your damp fabric in a plastic bucket and pour over the dye mix. Depending on the effect you want, keep moving the fabric to allow the dye take up to be even or scrunch or knot the fabric before placing in the dye bath for a more random effect. You can also use a spoon to splatter a different colour of dye over a different area of the fabric. The dye colours will eventually soak through and bleed into each other, creating new colour combinations.

5 Leave the fabric in the dye for at least 10 minutes, then carefully pour off the excess dye (this can be used for another fabric).

6 Mix three tablespoons of the soda solution to 850ml (30fl oz) of cold water and pour this into the bucket until the fabric is just covered.

7 Leave to fix for 30 minutes, then rinse the fabric under a cold tap until the water runs clear. There may always be a slight discharge of colour from home-dyed fabrics.

8 Leave the fabric to dry either by hanging it outside or using a tumble dryer. Avoid drying over a radiator as the heat is dispersed unevenly and you may get dark lines on your fabric. It also stiffens the fabric.

Fabric Directory

The following list provides a brief guide to the qualities and possible uses of all the fabrics chosen for the projects in this book. Each fabric is pictured on the opposite page.

1 Cotton Organdie
This comes in a wide range of colours and is relatively easy to work with in layered designs. Special effects can be created by carefully burning the edges. It tends not to fray badly but does not drape well.

2 Metallic Organdie
Useful for creating interesting and layered sheer effects. It works well for pintucks and reverse appliqué and interesting effects can be created by carefully burning sections away with a candle. Organdie is a fairly crisp fabric and does not drape well.

3 Twinkle Organdie
This delicate, sheer fabric has a slight sparkle and is often used for bridal gowns. It is useful for diffusing colour and for overlays.

4 Silk Chiffon
This has a soft delicate texture that drapes well. It is available in white for dyeing or in a range of ready-dyed colours. Chiffon is useful for layering up and fabric manipulation, but beginners may find it difficult to work with.

5 Dupion Silk
A flat woven dupion that comes in a wide range of colours, but it can be bought in white ready for dyeing. It is reasonably easy to work with but it does fray.

6 Shot Dupion Silk
A two-colour silk, available in a wide range of colour combinations, that looks different depending on the way the light strikes it. It is fairly easy to work with but it does fray.

7 Cotton and Polycotton
Widely available in a range of flat-dyed colours. Cotton, a natural fabric, has a medium drape, is easy to work with and does not fray too much. Pure cotton dyes well, which is useful as commercial dyed fabric colours tend to lack interest. Polycotton is a combination of cotton and man-made polyester.

8 Shot Rayon Velvet
Creates a luxurious look to projects, with a soft texture and drape. It is available in a wide range of colours. Note that velvet is difficult to work with when stitching together seams as the pile causes the fabric to slip.

9 Cotton Voile
A light-weight cotton with a soft texture. Good for diffused effects or as a background fabric. It dyes well and also comes in a range of pre-dyed colours.

10 Linen
A 100% natural fabric that comes in different weights. It crushes easily but is good to work with and can be dyed. Depending on the weight it may drape or be crisp. It is excellent for use in cutwork.

11 Felt
This thick fabric comes in a range of pre-dyed colours. It is useful for children's craft projects as it is stiff and does not fray. It has no drape. Hand-made pure felt can be dyed.

12 Aida
An embroidery fabric designed for cross-stitch projects and available in a variety of colours. Depending on the number of threads to the inch the finished project size may vary: the higher the count, the finer the fabric and the smaller the project. The fine counts may also be used for Hardanger embroidery.

13 Iron-on Interfacing
Iron-on interfacing comes in a variety of weights and textures. It is useful for stiffening fabric. There is a glue backing on one side of the interfacing that has to be fixed to the reverse of the chosen fabric with a hot iron.

14 Hardanger
A 22-count evenweave fabric, similar to Aida. It has a crisp texture. Once satin stitch blocks have been sewn, Hardanger blocks can be cut away and the fabric will not fray.

Materials and Equipment

Some of the equipment listed below may already be part of your basic sewing kit but it is worth investing a little more in certain items to ensure that they are of the best quality.

HOOPS

Hoops are used to hold fabric taut while machine embroidering and for hand embroidery. There are two main types, both consisting of an outer and inner ring.

Wooden hoops: the wooden hoops are the more traditional and do offer a reliable tension. They work best if the inner ring is bound with strips of cotton fabric as this helps prevent ring marks on the fabric as well as increasing grip.

Metal/plastic hoops: these are slimmer and fit neatly under an embroidery foot on the machine. They grip most fabrics well but shiny fabrics may slip and pucker whilst being sewn.

NEEDLES

Chenille needles: sharp pointed needles with a large eye. They are suitable for hand sewing thicker threads.

Embroidery needles: sharp pointed needles in a variety of sizes with a slightly larger eye than standard handsewing needles.

Handsewing needles: available in a variety of sizes and widths for sewing seams and basting.

Tapestry needles: blunt ended needles with a large eye that can easily be threaded with thick wool. The blunt end ensures the needle won't catch on the canvas threads while you are stitching.

Twin needle/triple needle: a double pointed needle for use in a domestic sewing machine. They are used to create beautiful textured effects, such as pin tucks. Two top threads are used for a twin needle, but only one bobbin thread.

THREADS

There is an enormous variety of threads on the market, available in various thicknesses and finishes from matt cotton to shiny rayon. Each type is best suited to a particular purpose. For hand embroidery choose stranded cotton, pearl cotton, or tapestry wool. These can be enhanced by blending filaments or by mixing with other threads for added texture and sheen. Machine projects can be worked in cotton or shiny rayon machine embroidery threads or machine silks. Try all threads on a sample before you commence any project and, where possible, refer to the manufacturer's instructions before proceeding.

SCISSORS

Dressmaking scissors: a good quality pair will last for years as they can be re-sharpened. They are available in different sizes and it is a good idea to try out before you buy in order to find a pair that feels right. Never use fabric scissors on paper and take care not to blunt them by accidentally cutting over pins.

Paper scissors: use any handy household scissors that are fairly sharp. Useful for cutting motifs and templates.

Small sharp pointed embroidery scissors: useful for trimming threads, motifs and layers of fabric. I prefer sharp pointed, small bladed scissors although there are scissors available with a small hook at the tip of one blade to allow for easy pick-up of fabric when working reverse appliqué.

SEWING MACHINE

A good domestic sewing machine usually performs a variety of functions. Most modern machines have a facility to convert to free machine embroidery, or the darning plate can be used. Try a variety of techniques on your machine before you buy.

TAPE MEASURE

A cloth tape measure provides accurate sizes for projects and templates and is more useful than a wind-up metal one for use with textiles.

IRON

A steam iron gives a crisp finish to embroidered projects, but never press hard on finished embroidery as it flattens the effect. Use a dry iron to bond small shapes.

PINS

Apart from their many uses, pins are essential for holding the different fabrics together in appliqué and also for pinning out water soluble embroidery. Use glass-headed pins for the projects as they are easier to find and remove.

Transferring Designs

There are a variety of ways of transferring designs onto fabric. Some of the projects have recommended methods although other options are available.

Tracing Directly onto Fabric

This is possible where the fabric you are using is transparent or light in colour (e.g. chiffon and voile). Simply lay the fabric on top of the template or motif, secure with masking tape, and trace using a pencil, water/air soluble fabric pen or tailors' chalk. Note that pencil lines will often not wash out so the project stitching has to cover it. With the water/air soluble fabric pen, some fabrics permanently stain although I've not come across this problem. The disadvantage in using tailors' chalk is that it rubs off easily and may disappear before the design is complete.

If you wish to trace onto the reverse of the fabric, note that this method will reverse the image. To avoid this you need to reverse the tracing paper and draw over the template lines before following the above method.

Tracing and Basting

Trace the design onto tissue paper or tracing paper and pin it to the fabric. Stitch the design outline by hand or by machine before carefully tearing away the tissue or tracing paper. The outline stitching will act as a guide for the embroidery. This method works best on dark or difficult to mark fabric such as velvet.

Light Box Tracing

This allows you to trace directly onto darker fabrics. Use masking tape to anchor the template or pattern to the light box then tape the fabric on top, right side up. Make sure the fabric is taut in order for it to be drawn upon. You can use pencil, water/air soluble fabric pen or tailors' chalk.

If you do not have access to a light box, tape the template and fabric to a brightly sunlit window, or make a simple light box by placing a table lamp under a glass topped coffee table. Alternatively, the glass from a picture frame positioned over a lamp would do – but be careful with this method.

Iron-on Transfers

Transfer pencils are available in craft shops and fabric shops and will give a permanent line on fabric. Begin by tracing the design onto tracing paper with an ordinary pencil. Then reverse the paper and carefully draw over the template lines using the transfer pencil. Now place the tracing (with the transfer pencil lines facing downwards) onto the right side of the fabric and press with a warm iron. Remove the paper to leave the tracing lines on the fabric.

Fusible Fabric Bond

An easy method of transferring designs for appliqué is to use fusible fabric bond. This is a thin glue that forms a web which can be ironed between two layers of fabric to stitch them together. It has a layer of waxed paper behind it in order to prevent it from sticking to the iron. Fabric bond is transparent and motifs can be traced through directly onto the paper backing before ironing onto fabric and trimming around a drawn mofit. Peel the paper backing off before ironing the motif onto the background fabric.

Enlargment and Reduction of Templates

You may need to enlarge or reduce a template or pattern. For information about this, see page 138.

Patterns

Printed on the next four pages are pattern pieces for the floral summer hat (see page 15) and the Chinese joss paper waistcoat (see page 87). These have all been reduced to 50% of their original size and will have to be enlarged. There are two main methods for enlarging (or reducing) a pattern or template: photocopying or the use of a grid.

Photocopying
If you have access to a good photocopy machine, the pattern pieces will need to be enlarged by 50%.

Grids
To use this method you need to trace or photocopy your original template or pattern, then draw a grid of equal squares – e.g. 2cm² (¾in²) – all over this original. Depending on whether you are enlarging or reducing your

design, draw another grid onto a separate sheet of paper. Use the same number of squares, but they must be larger or smaller than the original squares. To enlarge the patterns on these pages you will need to double the size of each square.

Now copy the lines of the first pattern onto the second grid. You will have to work freehand, but it is easy to use the squares as a guide to position the lines.

Points to note
• On pages 140/141, the waistcoat pattern has alignment points where the pattern has broken over the book's gutter. Match these up on your traced paper pattern before enlarging the pattern and cutting your fabric.

• Seam allowances are marked by dotted lines on all pattern pieces. All seams are 1.5cm (⅝in).

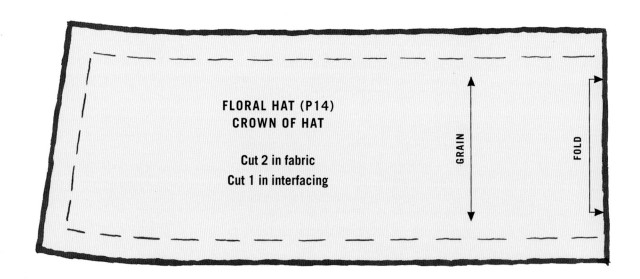

FLORAL HAT (P14)
CROWN OF HAT

Cut 2 in fabric
Cut 1 in interfacing

GRAIN

FOLD

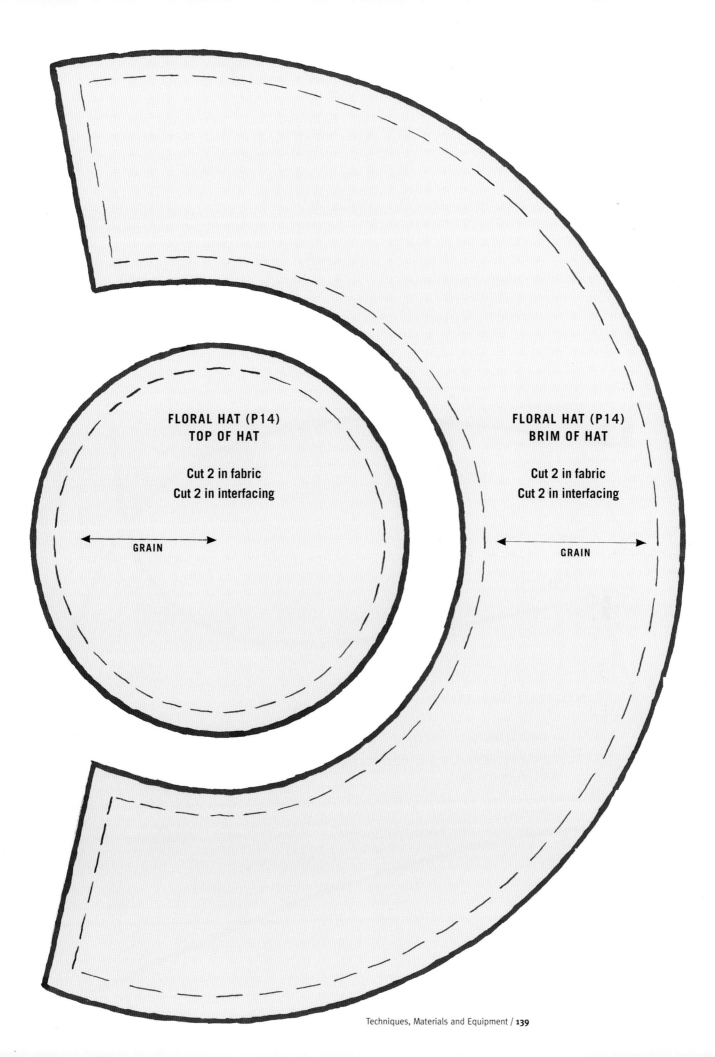

FLORAL HAT (P14)
TOP OF HAT

Cut 2 in fabric
Cut 2 in interfacing

GRAIN

FLORAL HAT (P14)
BRIM OF HAT

Cut 2 in fabric
Cut 2 in interfacing

GRAIN

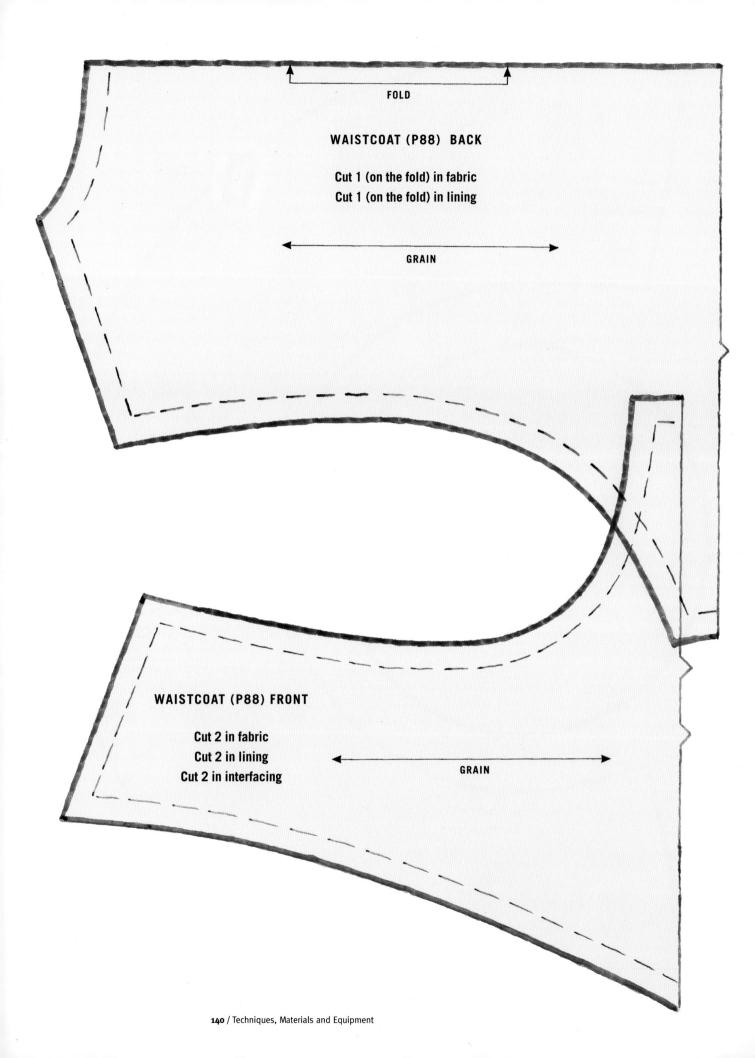

FOLD

WAISTCOAT (P88) BACK

Cut 1 (on the fold) in fabric
Cut 1 (on the fold) in lining

GRAIN

WAISTCOAT (P88) FRONT

Cut 2 in fabric
Cut 2 in lining
Cut 2 in interfacing

GRAIN

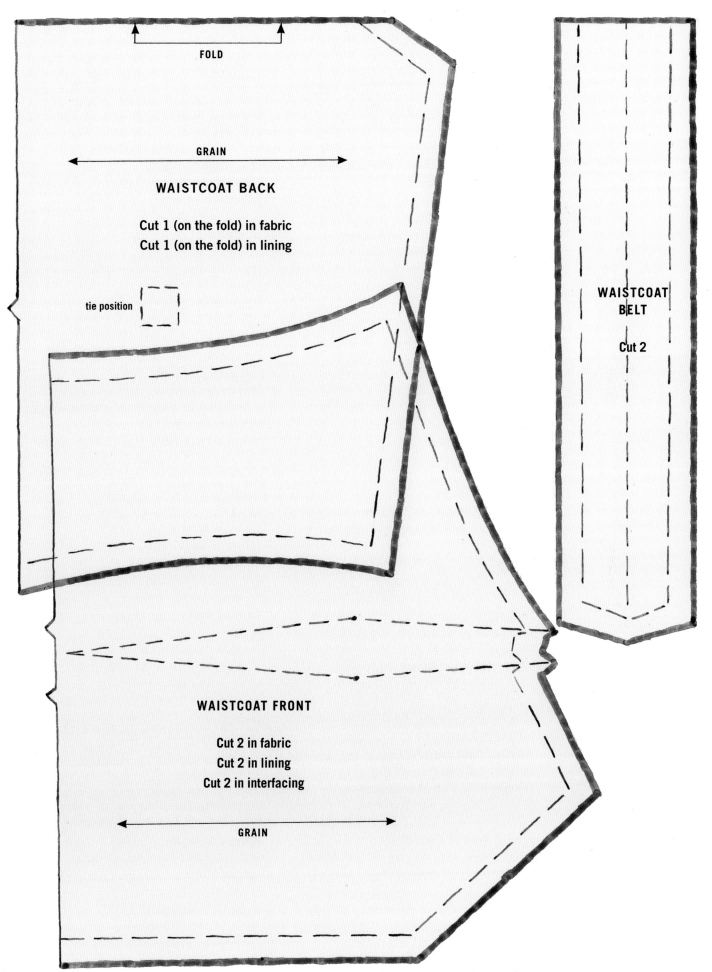

FOLD

GRAIN

WAISTCOAT BACK

Cut 1 (on the fold) in fabric

Cut 1 (on the fold) in lining

tie position

WAISTCOAT FRONT

Cut 2 in fabric

Cut 2 in lining

Cut 2 in interfacing

GRAIN

WAISTCOAT BELT

Cut 2

Glossary

Appliqué A method of applying one fabric onto a background fabric in a decorative manner

Baste Large running stitches used to mark guidelines on fabric or to stitch two fabrics together temporarily

Blocking A method of re-shaping distorted canvas work embroidery

Bobbin A sewing machine's bottom thread reel, used with the bobbin case to obtain the correct lower tension in the machine

Cutwork A technique that combines embroidered areas with cut areas to create a lacy or transparent effect. It may be simple or intricate

Darning/Embroidery foot A special foot attachment for a sewing machine that allows for multi-directional sewing (known as free machine embroidery)

Dart A pattern marking used in dressmaking that indicates an area to be stitched together in order to shape the finished garment

Diffused effect An effect created by layering white chiffon or organdie over an intensely coloured background. It softens the finished look

Embroidery hoop A wooden or plastic hoop that keeps fabric taut for correct tension during embroidery

Eyelets Fabric holes that are stitched around the edges to prevent them from fraying. Cords and ribbon can then be threaded through

Feed dog The zigzag teeth on the bed of a sewing machine that help feed the fabric through

Free machine embroidery A method of machine embroidery using a hoop and a darning foot that allows the embroiderer to stitch in any direction. It may also be done without a darning foot

Freestyle hand stitch A variety of stitches sewn by hand that may be used singly or combined

Fringing Describes when the horizontal threads are withdrawn from a fabric to leave a cut, frayed edge. It can be done using the point of a pin or a teazel

Fusible fabric bond An iron-on glue webbing useful for sandwiching two layers of fabric together (e.g. for appliqué techniques)

Hardanger A counted embroidery technique traditionally worked on a fine Aida type fabric. It is made up of blocks and cut areas

Interfacing A fabric stiffener that can either be sewn on or ironed on to give extra body to fabric. It also helps prevent fabrics from fraying

Light box A glass-topped metal box with internal strip lights that allow templates to be seen easily for tracing

Masking tape A form of sticky tape used to hold paper or fabric in place that can be peeled away afterwards

Overlocking Use of a stitch to finish raw edges and prevent them from fraying. Many domestic sewing machines now have a version of an overlock stitch

Pearl cotton A hand sewing thread that can be used for couching, cutwork and Hardanger techniques

Presser foot The foot on the sewing machine that guides the fabric through

Presser foot lever The bar that is pressed to activate the top tension and lower a sewing machine's presser foot

Shisha mirrors Indian glass mirrors used to decorate hand embroidery – machine embroidery shisha needs to be done using a plastic foil (e.g. coffee jar seals)

Skein A length of wool or thread as sold

Tack See **Baste**

Tailors' chalk A traditional chalk used to mark cloth which rubs off easily

Tail A loose thread end that must be trimmed or darned under

Tapestry wool A thick thread useful for canvas work

Teazel A natural, dried bristle brush or man-made metal brush used for fluffing up fabric or fraying edges

Template The trace-off diagrams given for a project

Three-dimensional embroidery The building up of a raised surface in embroidery

Twin needles Twin needles are available for most machines and allow for two parallel rows of stitching to be created simultaneously. Come in a variety of width settings

Water soluble fabric A fabric that dissolves in water after it has been embroidered to reveal a lacy stitched motif. It is available in either hot or cold water formats

Water/air soluble pen A fabric marker that helps define template lines. The marks can be washed out or left to vanish

Index

ACKNOWLEDGEMENTS

The author would like to thank the following people for their help and encouragement during the writing of the book:
  My husband Morph and son for being so understanding during the chaos.
  My parents, with love, for their support and babysitting services.
  My mum-in-law for typing up my scribbles with ease and cheerfulness.
  Also all the stitchers for interpreting my rather free sketches so well.
  Thanks to Sally and Julie at Coats for the threads and canvas, as well as to Mr and Mrs Deutsch, Jane and the staff at
    Mandors for all the sumptuous fabrics.
  Finally, a massive thank you to Caroline Bingham for patience and help throughout this book.

Designers:
Indian Bag: Toni Hanley, Bishopton, Glasgow
Brooches, Clasps and Waistcoat: Liz McLean McKay, Toronto, Canada

Stitchers:
Christine MacLeod, Karen Park, Theresa Lindsay,
Toni Hanley

Suppliers:
Coats Crafts UK
The Lingfield Estate
McMullen Road
Darlington
DL1 1YQ

Mandors Textile Centre
1 Scott Street
Glasgow
G3 6NU

Picture credits
All photography by **David Loftus** © Reed Consumer Books Limited, except
for the following:

Sandra Lane 72, 77 Top right, 96, 97 Bottom right, 97 Bottom left, 97
Top right, 97 Top left, 99 Bottom left, 99 Top, 99 Bottom right, 100,
101 Bottom right, 101 Top left, 111 Top right
Polly Wreford 77 Bottom right
Roger Stowell 101 Top right, 111 Centre right, 111 Top centre right
David Sherwin pages 116–135